Cleland, Elizabeth

A New and Easy Method of Cookery

ISBN: 978-1-948837-01-9

This classic reprint was produced from digital files in the Google Books digital collection, which may be found at http://www.books.google.com. The artwork used on the cover is from Wikimedia Commons and remains in the public domain. Omissions and/or errors in this book are due to either the physical condition of the original book or due to the scanning process by Google or its agents.

This edition of Elizabeth Cleland's **A New and Easy Method of Cookery** was originally published in 1755 (Edinburgh).

Townsends
PO Box 415, Pierceton, IN 46562
www.Townsends.us

A NEW AND EASY METHOD OF COOKERY

TREATING,

I. Of GRAVIES, SOUPS, BROTHS, *&c.*

II. Of FISH, and their SAUCES.

III. To Pot and Make HAMS, *&c.*

IV. Of PIES, PASTIES, *&c.*

V. Of PICKLING and PRESERVING.

VI. Of Made WINES, DISTILLING and BREWING, *&c.*

By ELIZABETH CLELAND.

Chiefly intended for the Benefit of the Young LADIES *who attend Her* SCHOOL.

EDINBURGH:
Printed for the Author by W. GORDON, C. WRIGHT, S. WILLISON and J. BRUCE:
And sold at Her House in the *Luckenbooths*.

M. DCC. LV.

THE
CONTENTS.

CHAP. I.

Of Gravies, Soups, Broths and Pottages.

CHAP. II.

Of dressing all Kinds of Fish, and their Sauces.

To

CONTENTS.

CHAP.

CONTENTS.

CHAP. III.

To pot and make Hams, &c.

To

C O N T E N T S.

CHAP.

CONTENTS.

CHAP IV.

To make Pies and Pasties, &c.

To

CONTENTS.

A

CONTENTS.

Maids

CONTENTS.

Macaroons

CHAP. V.

Of Pickling, and Preserving, &c.

Currants

CONTENTS.

CHAP. VI.

Of made Wines, &c.

A NEW AND EASY METHOD of COOKERY.

CHAP. I.

Of Gravies, Soups, Broths, and Pottages.

To make a ſtrong Broth for Soups or Sauces.

TAKE a Hough of Beef, or any coarſe Piece, and ſet it over the Fire, in four *Engliſh* Gallons of Water, ſkim it clean, ſeaſon it with Salt, whole Black and *Jamaica* Pepper, Mace, Cloves, a Bunch of ſweet Herbs, and ſix or ſeven Onions; boil it on a very ſlow Fire, for four Hours, then ſtrain it, and keep it for Uſe.

To make brown Gravy for Soups.

Cut three or four Pounds of coarſe Beef in thin Slices, put it in a Frying-pan, with a very little Piece of Butter, a ſliced Carot and Turnip, and Onions, with a Bunch of ſweet Herbs ; cover it cloſe, put it on a very ſlow Fire, fry it brown, but don't burn it ; then put to it ſome good Broth, then boil all together very well, and keep it for Soups or Sauces ; ſeaſon it with Pepper, Salt, *Jamaica* Pepper, and Cloves.

White Gravy for Soups or Sauces.

TAKE a Knuckle of Veal, and boil it in ſix *Engliſh* Quarts of Water, till it is in Strings, then ſtrain it ; but when it is half boiled, put in whole Mace, Pepper, Cloves, and Salt, ſo keep it for Uſe. You make Gravy of Mutton the ſame Way.

A good Stock for Fiſh Soups.

PREPARE Scate Flounders and Eels, lay them in a broad Gravy Pan, with a Sprig of Thyme, Parſley and Onions, ſeaſon them with Pepper, Salt, Cloves and Mace ; then pour in as much Water as cover them ; boil them on a very ſlow Fire for an Hour, then ſtrain it off: If it is for brown Soup or Sauces, put in the Skins of the Onions, and a brown Cruſt of Bread, with dried Muſhrooms ; keep the Gravy Pan cloſs covered.

A Vermicelli Soup.

TAKE three *Engliſh* Quarts of good Broth, put in it two Ounces of Vermicelli, and a Bit of lean Bacon, ſtuffed with Cloves ; put two Chickens or a boiled Fowl in it: You may make Rice Soup the ſame Way, but boil the Rice firſt in Water, then in Broth ; half an Hour boils the Vermicelli.

To make a Craw-fiſh or Lobſter Soup.

LET your Stock be as in Page firſt, take as many as will fill your Diſh, then take out the Sand-bags out of the Tails, and all the woolly Parts that are about them; put them in a Sauce-pan with your Soup, with Crumbs of Bread, and a little Butter; peel an Onion, ſtuff it with Cloves, and boil all the Shells in the Fiſh Stock, before you put in the Tail, and take them out when they are well boiled; ſtrain your Stock before you put in the Fiſh or any Seaſoning.

A Veal Soup with Barley.

YOUR Stock muſt be with a Fowl, and a Knuckle of Veal, ſeaſoned only with Mace, then ſtrain all off; put in half a Pound of fine Barley; boil it an Hour; ſeaſon it with Salt; put the Fowl in the Middle, and juſt as you ſerve it up, put in chopped Parſley.

A green Peaſe Soup.

TAKE a Peck of young green Peaſe, put them in a *Stew Pot*, cover them with Water, put in a little Thyme, Parſley, Onion, Pepper, Salt, and a good Lump of Butter; then cover them, and let them ſtew a While; then cut four Cabbage Lettices in Quarters, with ſix Cucumbers, pared and ſliced, and a Handful of Purſlain; put them in the Soup, with a Piece of Butter, and more ſeaſoning; then fill your Pan with Water; the Soup will take Stewing two Hours; if the Liquor is too much waſted away in that Time, add a little more boiling Water to it; you may put Slices of fried Bacon in the Diſh, or a roaſted Fowl if you pleaſe.

A brown Pottage Royal.

SET a Gallon of ſtrong Broth over the Fire, with two ſhivered Palates, Cocks Combs, Lambs Stones ſliced, with Forc'd-meat Balls, a Pint of Gravy, two Handfuls of Spinage, and young Lettice minced; boil theſe together with a Duck, the Leg and Wing being

being broke, and the Bones pulled out, and the Breaſt ſlaſhed, and browned in a Pan of Fat; then put the Pottage in a Diſh, and the Duck in the Middle; lay about it a little Vermicelli boiled up in ſome ſtrong Broth, with ſavoury Forc'd-meat Balls, and Sweetbreads; boil the Duck in the Broth for half an Hour before you diſh it.

Rice Soup.

TAKE a Quarter of a Pound of Rice, waſh it, boil it in Veal Broth till very tender, with a little Mace and a young Fowl; ſkim it very clean, and ſeaſon it with Salt to your Taſte; then ſtir in half a Pound of Butter, and a Mutchkin of Cream boiled up; then ſtir it in the Soup; ſerve it up with the Fowl.

Barley Pottage.

LAY a Pound of fine Barley to ſteep in two Chopins of Cream, ſome Salt, Mace and Cinnamon; when it is thick, ſweeten it to your Taſte.

A Pottage, forc'd Pigeons with Onions.

WASH and blanch them, take a Piece of Veal, a little Suet, pound them, and ſeaſon it with Pepper, Salt, Nutmeg, Lemon-peel, ſweet Herbs, Chives, Parſley, and Muſhrooms, all chopped ſmall; mix all together with Crumbs of Bread, and as many raw Eggs as will wet it; put it in your Pigeons, and ſtop their Vents; ſet them to boil in good Broth; take ſmall Onions, boil them and drain them, then put them to the Pigeons; take the Cruſts of fine Bread in ſome of the Broth, and put them in the Diſh under the Pigeons, and pour the Pottage on them.

To

To make Plumb Broth.

TAKE a good Hough of Beef, and a Knuckle of Veal, put it in the Pot with six *Scots* Pints of Water, boil it on a slow Fire; take up the Veal before it is too much, but boil the Beef to Pieces; if the Broth is too stiff, put in a Pint of boiling Water; put in the Crumbs of two Penny Loaves, two Pounds of Currants washed clean, two of Raisins stoned, one of Prunes, let all boil till they swell; season it with Salt, Cloves, Mace, and Nutmeg, strain the Broth before you put in the Fruit.

To make Spring Soup.

TAKE twelve Lettices, cut them in Slices, and put them into strong Broth, get six green Cucumbers, pare them, and cut out the Cores, cut them into little Bits, and scald them in boiling Water, and put them into your Broth; let them boil very tender, with a Mutchkin of young Pease and some Crumbs of Bread.

Pottage of Chervil the Dutch *Way.*

PUT into eight Chopins of good Broth a Knuckle of Veal, cut in Pieces the Bigness of an Egg, don't let it boil too fast, but keep it skim'd; season it with Pepper, Salt, Cloves and Mace, a Quarter of an Hour before you dish it; put in a good deal of Chervil chopp'd small, some Forc'd-meat Balls, and some Crumbs of Bread; let them boil well before you put them in, but not too much; so dish it.

Jelly Broth for consumptive Persons.

GET a Joint of Mutton, a Capon, a Fillet of Veal, put them in an Earthen Can close stopt, with three

Quarts

Quarts of Water; then put the Can in a Pot of Water, and when all the Flesh is boil'd to Rags strain it off for Use.

To make Soup de santé the French *Way.*

BOIL a Hough of Beef to Tavers on a very slow Fire; skim it, and when there is only what will fill your Dish, strain it; take three Pounds of Beef, cut in thin Slices, put it in a Pan with sliced Onions, Carots and Turnips in it, and a little Bit of Butter, till the Meat is brown, and the Pan dry; then pour your Soup on it, boil it an Hour, skim it and strain it; then get Chervil, Sorrel, Endive, Sellery, and Cabbage Lettices; cut them, but not too small, half boil them in Water, drain them, then put them in a close Goblet with your Soup; boil them till the Herbs are tender; season it with an Onion stuffed with Cloves, Pepper and Salt; put in the Dish a boiled Knuckle of Veal, or a Fowl, two *French* Rolls, the Crust only, or toasted Bread.

To make a Summer Pottage.

TAKE a Hough of Beef, a Scrag of Mutton or Veal, chop them, and boil them gently in a sufficient Quantity of Water for six Hours, being covered close, then put in four Onions, and whole Pepper; when the Meat is boiled to Rags, strain it, put in Cloves, Mace, and a Faggot of sweet Herbs, with Sorrel, Beets, Endive and Spinage, of each a Handful, shred grosly, boil it till they are tender; put it in the Dish with roasted Pigeons, or Ducks, in the Middle of it, and small Slices of fried Bacon, toasted Bread cut in Dice, Sausages cut in little Bits; in the Time of Asparagus, cut into Pieces the green Part, and boil them in it.

To make Meagre Broth for Soups with Herbs.

SET on the Fire a Kettle of Water, put in it ſome Cruſts of Bread, and all Sorts of Herbs, green Beets, Sellery, Endive, Lettice, Sorrel, green Onions, Parſley, Chervil, with a good Piece of Butter, and a Bunch of ſweet Herbs; boil it for an Hour and a Half, then ſtrain it off; this will ſerve to make Artichoke or Aſparagus, or *Soup de ſanté* with Herbs; ſeaſon it with Salt, Pepper, Cloves, *Jamaica* Pepper; cut the Herbs groſly, and it will be a very good Soup, boiling a good Lump of Butter with the Herbs, putting toaſted Bread in the Diſh; but take out the Bulk of the ſweet Herbs.

To make Scots *Barley Broth.*

BOIL a Hough of Beef in eight Pints of Water, and a Pound of Barley, on a ſlow Fire; let it boil to four Pints; then put in Onions, Pepper, Salt, and Raiſins if you like them, or you may put in Greens and Leeks.

A Calf's Head Soup.

TAKE a Calf's Head, ſtew it tender; then ſtrain off the Liquor, and put in a Bunch of ſweet Herbs, Onions, Salt, Pepper, Mace, and ſome fine Barley, boil it till the Barley and Head is done; then ſerve it with the Head in the Middle.

To make Mutton Broth.

TAKE about ſix Pounds of Mutton, boil it in three *Scots* Pints of Water, with ſweet Herbs, Onions, two or three Turnips, a Quarter of a Pound of fine Barley or Rice, Salt and Pepper; a little before you take it up, put in it a Handful of chopped Parſley.

To make another Barley Broth.

TAKE a Neck and Breaſt of Mutton, cut it to Pieces; put as much Water as will cover it; when it boils ſkim it; put in Barley, diced Carots, Turnips, Onions, a Faggot of Thyme and Parſley, Pepper and Salt, ſtove all well together; you may put in a Sheep's Head, but firſt ſinge and ſcrape it, and ſoak it well in Water; to make this green, put Beet Leaves, Brocoli, and green Onions, all ſhred ſmall.

A Purſlain Soup.

WHEN your Purſlain is young, cut the Sprigs off, but keep their whole Length; boil them in a Stew-pan, with ſome Peaſe-ſoup, and ſmall Onions; when your Purſlain is boiled in good Broth, put a Cruſt of Bread ſoaked in Broth in the Diſh, then pour your Soup on it with the Purſlain; ſeaſon it to your Taſte.

A Cucumber Soup.

PARE and ſlice them, not very thin, ſtew them in a little Butter, and put them in ſtrong Broth, ſeaſoned with Pepper, Salt and Onions; ſo ſerve them up.

To make Soup Meagre.

BOIL two or three Pounds of coarſe Beef in eight Chopins of Water, boil it to four; then ſtrain it off; then fry Slices of Carots, Turnips and Onions, in clarified Butter; drain them very well, put them in with Sorrel, Beets, Purſlain, Endive, Sellery, Cabbage-Lettice, of each a Handful; cut them groſly, and put them all in the Soup, with Cruſts of Bread, a Bunch of Parſley, green Onions and Thyme; ſeaſon it with Pepper

per, Cloves and Salt; after you put in your Herbs and Greens, boil them till the Roots are enough; boil the Roots and Sellery in it before you put in the rest.

An Eel Soup.

TAKE Eels according to the Quantity of Soup you would have; a Pound of Eels will make a Mutchkin of Soup; to every Pound of Eels add a Chopin of Water, a Crust of Bread, two or three Blades of Mace, whole Pepper, an Onion, and a Faggot of sweet Herbs; cover them close, and let them boil till Half the Liquor is wasted; then strain it, and put Toasts of Bread cut in Dice in the Dish, then pour on your Soup; you may put Forc'd-meat Balls made of Fish, or Bread, in it.

An Almond Soup.

YOUR Stock must be of Veal, blanch and beat a Pound of *Jordan* Almonds very fine, with the Yolks of six hard Eggs, putting a little cold Broth in as you pound them, then put in as much Broth as will fill the Dish; put it on the Fire, stir it often, then strain it off, and put in [illegible] small Chickens, and some Slices of fine Bread, season it with white Pepper, Mace and Salt, send it up hot.

Onion Soup.

TAKE Half a Pound of Butter, put it in a Stew-pan on the Fire, and boil it till it has done making a Noise; then take ten Onions, pared and cut small, throw them in the Butter, and let them fry a while, then shake in a little Flour, keep it stirring all the while, and let them do a little longer; then pour in three Mutchkins of boiling Water, stir them round, cut small the upper Crust of the stalest Penny Loaf you have, and put in it; season it with Pepper and Salt let it boil ten Minutes, take it off the Fire, beat the Yolks of two Eggs with Salt, a Spoonful of Vinegar, mix them, then ſtir it into the Soup; mix it well and diſh it.

A general Cullis for Fiſh.

WASH and ſcale ſome Carps, and cut them in Bits, put ſome Butter in a Pan, and place a good deal of Slices of Onions, and the Bill of the Carp in it, put it on a ſlow Fire, and when the Onions ſtick to the Bottom, put in ſome Peaſe Soup; put in a Sprig of Thyme, Parſley, Chives, Pepper, Cloves, and Mace; you may put in it a Clove of Rockambole or Garlick, if you like it; put a Lump of Butter into another Stew-pan, and put it on the Fire, with as much Flour as will thicken it; ſtir it till it is a light Brown, then put a little of the Carp Liquor in by Degrees, keeping it ſtirring all the Time; then pour all together with Anchovies, dry Muſhrooms, and Lemon-peel, with the Juice of it, and two Gills of white Wine; you may put in Gravy if you pleaſe: This Cullis will do for any Fiſh Soup or Cullis; you may make any Fiſh the ſame Way.

A Veal Cullis.

PUT in a Stew-pan a Piece of Butter, then cut Slices of Veal and lay them in it, with ſome Slices of a Carot, Turnip and Onions, and Slices of Ham if you like it; cover it cloſs, and when the Veal is brown take it out, and ſhake into your Pan a little Flour, keep it ſtirring with a Spoon till the Flour is brown; then put in ſome Broth by Degrees, keep it ſtewing all the while; if you have no Broth put in Water, put in as much as you will want then: put in the Veal with a Bunch of ſweet Herbs, whole Pepper, Mace, Onion ſtuffed with Cloves, and ſome Lemon-peel, let it ſtew well on a ſlow Fire, put in a Gill of white Wine, and when

when it is a good Brown, and the Veal well boiled in it, ſtrain it off; take off all the Fat, and you may uſe it with all Sorts of Entries.

Green Cullis for Soups or Sauces.

LET green Peaſe be done without Liquor, then take Parſley, Spinage, and green Onions, of each a Handful; blanch them, ſqueeze them well, and pound them, put in ſome Broth, with a Bit of Ham, an Onion ſtuffed with Cloves, ſome Slices of Veal, a Bunch of ſweet Herbs; your Peaſe and Veal muſt be ſtewed before you put in the Broth; and when clammy, put in the Broth and Juice of the Herbs, when all ſtews a while, take out the Meat, and pound the Peaſe, and then mix all together; ſeaſon it with Pepper, Salt and Mace, put in more green Parſley and green Onions, boil all; and when boil'd ſtrain it, it will ſerve in all green Soups and Sauces.

To make a brown Soup.

PUT in your Broth Pot a Hough of Beef, but firſt cut ſome of the beſt Pieces in thin Slices, ſkim your Pot, and let it boil very ſlow; fry your Steaks a little brown, and when your Broth is boiled, put it to your Steaks, with a little ſweet Herbs, two or three whole Onions, whole Black, and Clove Pepper and Cloves; before you put in your Ingredients, ſkim off all the Fat; you may put in Vermicelli in your Diſh, or Sellery with toaſted Bread; boil your Vermicelli and Sellery before you put it in your Soup; ſtrain your Soup before you put it to your fried Collops; put in your Broth by Degrees.

To make a white Soup.

BOIL a hind Leg of Lamb, Mutton or Veal, in Rags, then ſkim off all the Fat, ſeaſon it with Pepper, Cloves

Cloves and Mace, (they must be all whole) two or three whole Onions, and a Bunch of sweet Herbs; you may either whiten it with pounded Almonds or sweet Cream; strain it and salt it to your Taste, send the Shank in it to the Table.

To make Pease Soup.

BOIL a Hough of Beef, with a Pound and a Half of Pease, till they are all dissolved, then strain it and put in it whole Onions and Spice, salt it to your Taste, brown some Butter and Flour and mix with it: You may put boil'd Sellery cut in Dice in it, if you please. Take the whole Onions always out of every Thing; before it goes to the Table put Spearmint in it.

To make Onion Soup.

TAKE some of the Broth of a Hough of Beef, and boil in it a Dozen large Onions cut in Slices, with black and *Jamaica* Pepper, Salt, and a Bunch of sweet Herbs; thicken it with brown'd Butter and Flour and Crumbs of Bread; Take out your Herbs before it goes to the Table; let there be some small whole Onions boil'd in it.

Asparagus Soup.

TAKE some of the Broth of a Hough of Beef, and green it with the Juice of Spinage, cut half a Hundred of Asparagus, half an Inch long, and boil them in it, with black and *Jamaica* Pepper, an Onion stuffed with Cloves, and a Bunch of sweet Herbs, thicken it with Flour and Butter, boil it well after you put in the Butter and Flour.

To make Hodge-podge.

BOIL a Neck and Breaſt of Mutton in three Quarts of Water, ſkim it well, then put in Turnips and Carots cut in Dice; if they are old, boil them in Water firſt, when it is almoſt boil'd put in ſome Crumbs of Bread, two Onions, and a Chopin of green Peaſe, thicken it with brown'd Butter and Flour, put in it a brown'd Cruſt of Bread, Pepper and Salt; you may put in Sellery or Endive if you pleaſe; Brocoli or Aſparagus is very good in it, when you can't get Peaſe; take out the Cruſt of Bread before you ſend it to Table.

To make a green Peaſe Soup.

BOIL a Peck of Peaſe into two Quarts of Water till they are all in Smaſh, keep out a Mutchkin of the youngeſt, put them in a little before you diſh them; ſtrain and rub your Peaſe thro' a Search, then put it on the Fire again, and put a little Juice of Spinage in it, and a little Spearmint, Pepper and Salt to your Taſte, Half a Pound of Butter work'd in Flour, then your green Peaſe: Let it boil till you think it thick enough, and then ſerve it up. If you have a Mind to have it rich, inſtead of Water, put the Broth of a Hough of Beef, with a good white Gravy, in it.

A very good Peaſe Soup.

BOIL three Pounds of lean Beef in eight Chopins of Water, and three Pound of Peaſe, till the Meat is all in Rags, then put in two or three Anchovies, a Faggot of Thyme, Spearmint, Parſley, and Ginger, Pepper, Salt and Cloves, with ſome Onions; then boil it for a while, and ſtrain it off in a clean Pan, then give it another Boil, ſtirring in it a good Piece of Butter. Fry ſome Forc'd-meat Balls, Bacon cut in thin Slices, and

Bread cut in Dice, with Spinage boil'd green and chopped small, with a Bit of Butter and Salt, and roll'd in Balls: Put all in the Dish, and pour the Soup boiling hot over them.

To make a Pottage the French *Way.*

TAKE hard Lettices, Sorrel, Chervil, Beets and Spinage, of each a like Quantity, or any other Herbs you like, as much as a Half Peck will hold pressed down; pick, wash and drain them, put them in a Pot with a Pound of fresh Butter, and set them over the Fire, and, as the Butter melts, stir them down in it till they are as low as the Butter, then put in some Water; season it with Pepper, Cloves and Salt, put in a Crust of Bread, and some Chives, and when it is boil'd, take out the Bread, and thicken it with the Yolks of three or four Eggs, take Care they don't curdle, beat them well, put Toasts of Bread in the Dish with it.

To make Pottage of chopped Herbs.

MINCE, very fine, Spinage, Chives, Parsley, Marigold-flowers, Succory, Strawberry and Violet Leaves, stamp them with Oat-meal in a Bowl, put chopped Greens in with it; you may either put Broth or Water to them; if Water, boil a good Piece of Butter in it; put Sipets in the Dish, and pour it over them.

A Fish Broth.

CUT Carots, Turnips and Onions, in thin Slices, put them into a Stew-pan with a Lump of Butter; when they are brown put to them some Fish Broth, made of either Carps, Eels, Haddocks or Scate, then put in Parsley, Thyme, Chives, and some dry Mushrooms; season it with Pepper, Salt and Cloves; boil it an Hour with a Crust of Bread in it.

An Oister Soup.

TAKE a Chopin of Oisters, wash them clean in their own Liquor, then strain the Liquor, put to it two Gills of Water and one Gill of white Wine, a Sprig of Thyme and Parsley, a Shalot, a Bit of Lemon-peel, a few Cloves, a Blade of Mace, and some whole Pepper, let them stew gently for a little ; put a Quarter of a Pound of Butter into a Pan, flour it well, then let it fry till it has done hissing, keep it stirring; then take the Oisters and dry them in a Cloth, and flour them, put them in the boiling Butter, and fry them till they are plump, then put in their own Liquor, with three Mutchkins of strong Broth, keep it stirring all the Time : If your Soup is not brown, you may put Toasts in the Dish cut in Dice, and a *French* Loaf toasted.

To make Calves-feet Broth.

BOIL the Feet in just as much Water as will make a good Jelly, then strain it, and set the Liquor on the Fire, putting in two Blades of Mace, put in two Gills of Malaga, and Half a Pound of Currants, wash'd and pick'd ; and when they are plump'd, beat up the Yolks of two Eggs, and mix them with a little of the cold Broth, and thicken it over a slow Fire, keeping it stirring all the while one Way : Season it with Salt, Sugar, Nutmeg, boil in it the Rind of a Lemon, and just before you dish it put in it the Juice of a Lemon.

Broth of Roots.

BOIL three Pounds of good white Pease ; when they are very tender, bruise them to a Mash, put them into a Pot that holds six Chopins of Water, put it on the Fire for an Hour, strain it off and rub the Pease thro' a Sieve ; then put it in a Pan with a Bunch of sweet Herbs,

Herbs, a shred Carot, six Onions, Parsley Roots, Sorrel, Chervil, Lettice, Endive and Sellery, a Handful of each: Season it with Salt, Pepper, Cloves, and *Jamaica* Pepper; boil it very well, it will be very good to put in any Herb Soup, or for a Soup with toasted Bread in it.

To make Cake-soup.

TAKE a Hough of Beef, a Knuckle of Veal, strip off the Skin and Fat, then take all the muscular and fleshy Parts from the Bones, boil the Flesh gently in three *Scots* Pints of Water, for so long a Time till the Liquor will make strong Jelly; try it if it is very strong before you strain it, by putting some to cool; strain it through a Sieve and let it settle, then let it be put in white Stone Cups, as clear as you can from the Settling, and set them in a Pan of cold Water, and put them on a slow Fire, and let the Water boil gently, till the Jelly is as thick as Glue; take Care the Water does not go into the Cups, then let them stand to cool, and then turn out the Glue upon a Piece of Flannel, keep them turned every eight Hours on a dry Place of the Flannel till they are quite dry; then paper them in white Papers, and hang them up in a dry Place; there must be but one in every Paper: When you are going to make Use of them, boil an *English* Quart of Water, and pour it on them, keeping it stirring all the Time till it dissolves, it will make good Soup; season it to your Taste with Pepper, and put no Seasoning in the Glue; you may carry it in your Pocket, it will be good for Gravy or Sauce.

A Pottage of Goose Giblets.

SCALD and wash them clean, and cut them in Pieces, season them with Pepper, Salt, Onions, and a Bunch of sweet Herbs, boil them in good Broth till they are very tender, with some Crusts of

Bread

Bread in it; you may put green Peaſe and ſliced Lettices in it, take out the Herbs before you diſh them.

A Muſſel Soup.

GET a Pint of Muſſels, ſcald them and waſh them clean, put them in a Pan with three Mutchkins of ſtrong Broth, and a Mutchkin of their own Liquor, a Bunch of ſweet Herbs, an Onion ſtuffed with Cloves, Pepper, Mace and Salt, put in Crumbs of Bread to thicken it, you may put a Gill of white Wine in it; boil it till it is ſmooth, you may ſqueeze in it a little Lemon Juice, ſo ſerve it up hot.

A Peaſe Soup with Herbs in it.

BOIL two Pounds of Peaſe in ſix Chopins of Water till they are very ſoft, pour off ſome of the Liquor, and rub the Peaſe thro' a Sieve, ſtill putting in ſome of the Liquor to make them go through; then boil a Pound of Butter, and when it breaks in the Middle, put in an Onion and a little Mint cut ſmall, Spinage, Sorrel, and Sellery cut groſly, let them boil a while, ſtirring them often; then with one Hand ſhake in ſome Flour, while with the other you pour in the thin Liquor; then ſtir all together, ſeaſon it with Pepper, Mace and Salt, boil it for an Hour longer, then diſh it: You may put in a little ſweet Cream if you pleaſe.

To make Peaſe Pottage.

TAKE two Quarts of Peaſe, put them into three Quarts of Water, ſeaſon it pretty high with Pepper and Salt, boil them till they are enough, mix a Spoonful of Flour with Water, and put in a little Mint, a Leek, two Handfuls of Spinage, all cut ſmall; put in Half a Pound of Butter, boil it and diſh it.

A Turnip Soup.

PARE and cut in Dice twelve Turnips, which will make a Diſh full, fry them in clarified Butter a light brown, put them in two Chopins of good Gravy and the Crusts of fine Bread, let them drain from the Fat, boil them till tender: You may put a Fowl in the Middle.

A Hare Soup.

CUT your Hare in Quarters, and the rest in small Pieces, put it in a Stew-pot with a Crag or Knuckle of Veal; put in a Gallon of Water, a Bunch of sweet Herbs, let it stew till the Gravy is very good, fry a little of the Veal and put in it to make it brown, put in Bread to thicken the Soup, or you may put in Rice, but boil it first a little, or fine Barley, a Quarter of a Pound of either will do; season it with Pepper, Salt, and Mace, with an Onion stuffed with Cloves; take out the Herbs, Veal and Onion, before you dish it.

CHAP. II.

Of dressing all Kinds of FISH, *and their Sauces.*

To stew Carp or Tench.

WHEN they are catch'd put them in a Tub of Water, kill them and save all their Blood, scrape them, salt them well to take off the Slime, then wash and dry them very well in a Cloath: If they are small, fry them first, stew them in a Mutchkin of Claret, and the same of Gravy, a Piece of Butter work'd in Flour, Pepper, Cloves, Salt and Mace, a whole Onion, a Bunch of sweet Herbs, and an Anchovy, if you have them; put Truffles, Morels, and Oisters in it, boil the Truffles, and Morels, scald and pick the Oisters: Let your Sauce be boil'd, then put in your Fish and stew them a good while, but don't let them

break;

break: If the Sauce wants it, put in Ketchup; the large ones put in without frying, and ſtew them on a very ſlow Fire, there muſt be more Claret and Gravy in theſe than the fried ones; brown the Butter and Flour that you put in them that are not fried.

To dreſs a Cod's Head.

IF you boil it, let your Water be boiling, put in it a Handful of Salt, a little Vinegar, and then put in your Fiſh, be ſure the Water covers it; if large, it will take an Hour to boil it; if ſmall, Half an Hour; the ſame Time bakes it, if the Oven is very hot: If baked, put Butter over and under it, the Sauce muſt be either Oiſters, Shrimps or Lobſters. Garniſh the Diſh with Parſley, Horſe-radiſh, and Forc'd-meat Balls, and ſliced Lemon.

To make Oiſter, Lobſter or Shrimp Sauce.

PICK your Oiſters clean and ſcald them, ſtrain their own Liquor and put it on them, then put Gravy if you have it, or a little Water in it; put in it a good Piece of Butter worked in Flour, a whole Onion, the Rind of a Lemon, Pepper, Salt, Nutmeg, and the Juice of Half a Lemon, you may put in Ketchup if you have it. The Lobſters muſt be cut in Pieces, and white Wine in it.

To roaſt or bake a Salmon.

SCORE it on the Back, ſeaſon it with Salt, Pepper, Mace and Nutmeg; put grated Bread, the Grate of a Lemon, Parſley, Thyme, Salt and Butter in every Score, and in the Belly; put it in a cloſe cover'd Pan in the Oven, with ſome Butter on the Top and Bottom. You may give it either Oiſter or Lobſter Sauce, or plain Butter.

To pickle Salmon.

TAKE a whole Salmon, and ſcrape it clean, don't waſh it, cut it in round Pieces two Inches thick, ſtrew Salt

Salt on it to purge out the Blood. Make a ſtrong Pickle of Salt and Water, whole Pepper, Mace and Cloves, with a Mutchkin of Vinegar and ſix Bay Leaves; when it boils put in the Salmon, and let it boil a Quarter of an Hour; then take it out, and ſet the Pickle to cool, ſkim all the Greaſe off it, then put in your Salmon. You may do large Trouts or Pikes the ſame Way; if your Salmon is very thick, it will take more boiling.

A Turbet or any flat Fiſh in Jelly.

WHEN your Fiſh is well clean'd, let it lye in Salt two Hours, then waſh it and boil as much Water as will cover it; put in your Water Two-pence Worth of Iſinglaſs, Salt, Cloves, Mace and Pepper, and a Gill of Sherry, and one of Vinegar; put in your Fiſh when the Liquor boils, and when you think it is enough, take it out and put on the Liquor again, and let it boil till it jellies; then beat the Whites of three Eggs and put in it, and give it four or five Boils more, then run it thro' a Jelly Bag, put your Fiſh on the Diſh, and when it is almoſt cold, pour it on, Lemon Juice being better than Vinegar, and boil the Rind in it.

To broil Salmon.

BROIL ſome Pieces of Salmon, ſeaſoned with Pepper and Salt; for the Sauce, put Butter, and Duſt of Flour, a green Onion, an Anchovy, a little Ketchup, Oiſter Liquor, a Glaſs of white Wine, and the Juice of a Lemon; ſeaſon it with Pepper, Salt, Nutmeg, and the Grate of a Lemon; diſh your Salmon, and pour your Sauce about it; you may dip the Pieces of Salmon in melted Butter, and ſtrew on them Crumbs of Bread and ſweet Herbs ſhred ſmall, before you broil it. and the ſame Sauce.

To farce Slices of Salmon.

CUT Slices of Salmon an Inch thick, take off the Skins, then mince ſome of the Salmon, with ſome Eels, Muſhrooms,

rooms, Chives and Parſley; ſeaſon it with Pepper, Salt, Nutmeg, Cloves and Lemon-peel, pound them with a Piece of Butter; then put in it ſome Crumbs of Bread, and wet it with Eggs; dip the Salmon in Butter, and lay the Farce all over them; lay ſome Butter in a Diſh, lay your Salmon in it, and cover it cloſs; put it in the Oven; when baked, put it in the Diſh, with either Oiſter, Lobſter, or Cockle Sauce.

To haſh Salmon.

HASH ſome Salmon in a Sauce-pan, dry it over the Fire till it grows white; then mince ſmall ſome Muſhrooms, Parſley, Shrimps and Oiſters, and mince them all together; put ſome Butter in a Pan, with a little Flour; keep it ſtirring till it is brown; then put in the Salmon, give it a Turn or two on the Fire, ſeaſon it with Salt and Pepper, and a little Juice of Lemon; put in a little Broth; ſerve it up hot.

To fry Salmon.

TAKE a Chine, or any other Part of Salmon, and cut it in Pieces, and fry them in clarified Butter or Beef Drippings, a little brown and criſp: For Sauce, put in the Sauce-pan ſome Claret, a Piece of Butter work'd in a little Flour, ſome Oiſter Liquor, the Juice of Lemon, and Nutmeg; put it on the Fire, and keep it ſtirring; diſh the Fiſh, and pour it over them.

To bake a Turbot.

LAY ſome Butter in a Diſh, the Size of the Turbot, and put Butter all over it; ſeaſon it with Pepper, Salt, Cloves and Nutmeg, Crumbs of Bread, Lemon-peel, Chives, Parſley, a little Thyme, all ſhred ſmall; flour it all over with it, bake it in the Oven a light brown, ſend it to the Table dry, with two Sauce-boats, one with Butter, the other with Oiſter Sauce.

To fry a Turbot.

SCORE your Turbot, flour it and fry it in clarified Butter, or good Beef Drippings; let it be boiling hot; then put it in, and fry it a good brown, then drain it; make the Pan clean, put in it Claret or white Wine, Anchovy, Nutmeg, and an Onion, ſtuffed with Cloves and a little Salt; then put in your Fiſh, and let it boil a good While; then put in a Piece of Butter, work'd in a little Flour, and ſome Lemon-peel, mix it well: Put your Fiſh in the Diſh, and pour the Sauce over it, but take out the Onion.

To ſouſe a Turbot.

BOIL it in Salt and Water, as much as will cover it, with a Mutchkin of Vinegar, Lemon-peel, Ginger, whole Pepper and Cloves; when boiled take it out, and when it and the Liquor is cold, put it in again with ſome Bay Leaves, and it will be fit to eat in two Days.

To ſtew a Turbot.

CUT it in Slices, and fry them; when they are half done, put them in a Stew-pan, with Claret, Lemon Juice, a ſliced Onion, Nutmeg, and a Bit of Butter; let the Fiſh ſtew till done; diſh it.

To cramp Cod the Dutch *Way.*

BOIL four Chopins of Water, and a Pound of Salt, ſkim it well; then put in the Slices of Cod; when it has boiled three Minutes it is done; then drain them well, and diſh them with raw Parſley about them; they muſt be cut very thin; they are eaten with Oil, Muſtard and Vinegar.

To ſtew Soals or any flat Fiſh.

SKIN your Soals, if they are large, on both Sides, and cut them in the Middle; if ſmall, leave them whole, and ſkin them of the black Skin, the other

Fiſh

Fish is not to be skinned, have a Pan full of clarified Butter or Beef, or Beef Dripping, boiling hot; flour your Fish and put them in, fry them a light brown, then put them to drain all the Fat from them; brown a good Piece of Butter and Flour, and put to it some Gravy, Oister Liquor, a Bunch of sweet Herbs, an Onion or two, Cloves, Mace, Pepper and Salt, half a Mutchkin of Claret, the Juice of a Lemon, and a chopped Anchovy; when they are well mix'd together put in your Fish, and let them simmer over a very slow Fire; if it is not thick enough, work a Bit of Butter in Flour and put in it; half an Hour stews them: You may put Truffles and Morels in them; take out the Herbs and Onions, garnish your Dish with sliced Lemon.

To boil a Turbot or any flat Fish.

PUT in your Fish-kettle as much Water as will cover the Fish, a Handful of Salt, two Gills of Vinegar, and a Stick of Horse-radish; put your Fish in when the Water boils; an Hour boils a Turbot; the small Fish less; you may give them Oister, Lobster, or Shrimp Sauce: Garnish the Dish with Parsley, sliced Lemon, and Horse-radish; let your Fish lye in Salt and Water ten or twelve Hours before you boil it: If you souse your Fish, you must put in more Vinegar, Pepper, Cloves, Mace, Salt, and Bay Leaves; take out your Fish, then boil your Liquor better, put in whole Ginger and Lemon-peel, it will make your Liquor better; and when both is cold pour the Liquor on your Fish: It is to be eaten cold with Oil, Vinegar and Mustard, or with some of its own Liquor; you may put *French* white Wine in it with Vinegar. You may souse Pike the same Way.

To roast or bake a Pike.

SCORE your Pike on the Back, rub it all over with melted Butter; make a Stuffing of Crumbs of Bread,

Oisters,

Oisters, Lemon-peel, Parsley, Shalot, Thyme, sweet Marjoram, and Anchovies, all shred small; put in as much Beef Sewet finely chopped, as Bread; season it with Pepper, Salt, Cloves and Nutmeg; wet it with two Eggs, and lay a Lair of it in every Score, and put some in the Belly: Strew on the Fish Crumbs of Bread, Pepper, Salt, the Grate of a Lemon and Nutmeg, roll it up in the Caul of Veal or Lamb, or a very thick buttered Paper; tye it to a Spit and flame it well with Butter, or turn it round in a Dish, and put Butter about it. Put it in the Oven, and when done, drain all the Gravy from it, and make a Lobster or Oister Sauce for it; or you may take a little Gravy, a Piece of Butter work'd in Flour, an Onion stuffed with Cloves, a Gill of red or white Wine, the Gravy that comes out of the Fish, Oister Liquor, and Ketch-up. Garnish the Dish with fried Parsley, sliced Lemons, and shred Beet-roots and Pickles.

To make Oister Loaves.

GET five little *French* Loaves, cut a little round Bit out of the Top, and take out all the Crumbs, fry the Crusts, and boil them in clarified Butter: Take half a Hundred of large Oisters, scald and wash them very clean, crum the Pith of the Loaves, and put some of it in the Oisters; strain the Liquor to them; put grated Lemon and Nutmeg, a good Piece of Butter, a little Pepper, stir this in a Toss-pan on the Fire till it is very hot; then stir in a little white Wine, and a little Juice of Lemon, then fill your Loaves with it, let both be hot; put the Bit you cut off the Top on it again; you may make it without the Crumbs; thicken the Oisters with a little Cream and the Yolks of Eggs.

To dress a Pike with Oisters.

SCALE and gut it, wash it clean, cut it in Pieces, and put them in a Stew-pan with a Gill of white Wine, a Half Mutchkin of Water, Half a Gill of Vinegar, Parsley, Chives, Mushrooms if you have them, and Truffles;

Truffles, Morels, and blanch'd Oisters, with their own Liquor, a Piece of Butter work'd in Flour, Pepper, Salt, Mace and Nutmeg; boil them all together, with a Bunch of sweet Herbs, and an Onion and Parsley must be shred.

To souse a Pike.

PUT the Pike into as much Water as will cover it, with Bay Leaves, Pepper, Cloves, Mace and Salt: Let it boil till it is tender, that a Straw may run thro' it; then take it up and put in the Liquor white Wine and Vinegar: When your Liquor is cold put in your Fish. When it goes to the Table, garnish it with pickled Barberries, Lemon and Parsley; put some of its own Liquor about it.

To boil a Pike.

THRUST the Tail of the Pike in its Mouth, boil as much Water as will cover it; put in it a Gill of Vinegar, the Juice and Rind of a Lemon, a Piece of Horse-radish, put a Stuffing of Forc'd-meat made of Fish in the Belly; and when the Water boils, put in your Fish, and boil it with a quick Fire: For the Sauce, take a little of the Liquor it is boil'd in, an Onion stuffed with Cloves, the Liver minc'd, a Bunch of sweet Herbs, Pepper, Mace and Salt, put in Oisters or Cockles blanched, and pour on Liquor, a good Piece of Butter worked in Flour, a little white Wine and Ketchup; garnish it with Pickles and sliced Lemon.

To fry a Pike.

CUT it in Slices, put in it Verjuice, Salt, Pepper, Lemon Juice, Chives and Bay-leaves; let it lye Half an Hour, then dip them in a Batter and fry them; dish them garnish'd with slic'd Lemons and Parsley: Make your Sauce of brown'd Butter and Flour, Oister Liquor, Mushroom Liquor, Gravy of Fish or Flesh, Pepper, Salt and Mace, a little white Wine, and Lemon Juice.

D *To*

To bake Plaice or any flat Fish.

CUT off the Heads, Tails and Fins; season them with Salt, Pepper, Nutmeg and Cloves, Parsley, sweet Herbs, Lemon-peel, Anchovies and Shalots, put Butter under and over them; strew on them Crumbs of Bread, bake them a fine Brown, cut all the Ingredients small; you may put in either Oisters, Cockles, or Shrimps, a Gill of white Wine, and the Juice of a Lemon. If the Dish is a handsome Dish you bake them in, you may send them to Table in it, if not, take Care in taking them out; you may send them, as they are baked, with either plain Fish Sauce, or Lobster, or Shrimp.

To stew Soals.

PUT your Soals in a Stew-pan, with two Gills of white Wine, whole Pepper, Mace, Lemon-peel and Salt; when they are half-stewed, put in a little Butter work'd in Flour, stir it till it is melted; then put in some Oisters and their own Liquor, keep them often shaking till the Fish is enough. Squeeze in a little Juice of Lemons: Garnish the Dish with Lemon, and fried Toasts of Bread.

To boil Mullets, or stew them.

BOIL your Water and Salt, just as much as will cover them; then put in your Fish, with Vinegar and Horse-radish; take them up and let them drain, boil some of their own Liquor, a Bunch of sweet Herbs, Onions, Pepper, Salt, Lemon-peel and Nutmeg, Ketchup, white Wine and Lemon Juice, thicken it with Butter and Flour; so serve them up, garnished with red Cabbage, scraped Horse-radish, and sliced Lemon.

To pickle Smelts.

YOUR Fish being washed and gutted, dry them in a Cloth; lay them in Rows, and put between every Row, Pepper, Nutmeg, Cloves, Mace and Salt, with the Powder of Cochineal, Salt-petre and Peter-salt; co-

ver

ver them with Bay Leaves, then boil as much Vinegar as will cover them, and when cold pour it on them.

To roſt a Cod's Head.

SCORE it with a Knife, and ſtrew a little Salt on it, and lay it in a Stew-pan before the Fire, with ſomething behind it, throw away the Water that runs out of it the firſt half Hour; then rub it over with a little Butter, and ſtrew on it Nutmeg, Cloves, Mace and Salt; turn it often and baſte it with Butter: If it is a very large Head, it will take four Hours roſting; take all the Gravy that runs out of it, and put more Gravy to it, and a Glaſs of white Wine, three Shalots, a little Horſe-radiſh, Pepper, Cloves, Mace, Salt and Nutmeg, a good Lump of Butter worked in Flour, the Liver of the Fiſh boiled, and chopped with Anchovies very ſmall, ſome Oiſters and Shrimps; thicken it with the Yolks of two Eggs, juſt as you're going to put it in the Sauce-boat. Lay your Cod's Head on the Diſh, and put ſmall fried Fiſh and Forc'd-meat Balls, Slices of Lemons, Horſe-radiſh and Pickles over it, and ſend it up very hot.

To ſtew Cod.

CUT the Cod in thin Slices, lay it in a Diſh with a Mutchkin of Gravy, and two Gills of white Wine, ſome Oiſters and their Liquor; ſeaſon it with Pepper, Salt and Nutmeg, and let it ſtew till it is almoſt enough, then thicken it with a Piece of Butter roll'd in Flour, let it ſtew a little longer: Put in the Juice of a Piece of Lemon; ſerve it up very hot.

To broil a Cod.

CUT the Cod in middling Pieces about an Inch thick, flour it well, and put it on the Gridiron over a ſlow Fire: The Sauce is a little Gravy, a Glaſs of white Wine, an Anchovy, Pepper, Salt, an Onion ſtuffed with Cloves, a Spoonful of Walnut Liquor; boil the Liver, chop it ſmall, and a Piece of Butter rolled

rolled in Flour in the Sauce; you may put in Oisters, Shrimps or Mushrooms; see that your Fish is well broil'd: Dish it, and put Parsley about it. Send your Sauce in a Boat.

To dress a Cod's Tail.

LOOSE the Skin that it may fall from the Flesh; take the Fillets out, and make it with more Fish in Forc'd-meat, and fill up the void Spaces; then put the Skin upon the Tail again, rub it with Butter, and strew on it Crumbs of Bread, Pepper, Salt, and Lemon-peel, sweet Herbs shred small: Then put it in the Oven, and bake it a light Brown. You may make a Ragoo for it, or give it any Fish Sauce you please.

To stew Carps à la Royale.

WHEN they are very clean, put them in Claret, Salt, Pepper, Lemon-peel, an Onion stuffed with Cloves, Horse-radish, and a little Vinegar; cover them clos, and let them stew gently on a slow Fire for three Quarters of an Hour; then beat some Butter, some of the Liquor that the Fish is stewed in, with two Anchovies chopped small, and some Oisters. Dish your Carps on Sippets, and pour the Sauce over them.

To boil Carps.

SAVE the Blood, then boil them in a good relished Liquor for half an Hour; make the Sauce of the Blood, Claret, and good Gravy, two Anchovies, two Shalots, whole Pepper, Cloves and Mace. Let all stew together; thicken it with Butter rolled in Flour, grate Nutmeg in it, and a little Lemon Juice; salt it to your Taste; drain your Fish well: Dish them, and pour the Sauce boiling hot over them.

To dress Eels with white Sauce.

SKIN and cut them in Pieces, blanch them, then dry them in a Napkin; toss them up in Butter, with

Salt,

Salt, Pepper, Cloves, Lemon-peel, and a Glaſs of white Wine: Toſs up likeways ſome Artichoke Bottoms, Muſhrooms and Aſparagus, with Butter and ſavoury Herbs: Thicken the Sauce with the Yolks of Eggs; ſo ſerve them: Put Slices of Lemon and a little Juice in it.

To dreſs Eels with brown Sauce.

CUT your Eels in Pieces, toſs them up in clarified Butter and Flour; then put to them a little Fiſh Broth, Chives and Parſley ſhred ſmall, ſome Muſhrooms and Capers, a Bunch of ſweet Herbs, an Onion ſtuffed with Cloves, Pepper and Salt. When well boiled, put in a Glaſs of white Wine, and the Squeeze of a Lemon, and the Yolk of an Egg with Butter. So ſerve it up hot.

To fry Eels.

SKIN them, bone them, and cut them in Pieces, and lay them in Vinegar, Salt, Pepper, Bay Leaves, ſliced Onions, for two Hours; then drudge them with Flour, and fry them in clarified Butter. Serve them up dry with fried Parſley.

To dreſs Eels à la Daube.

MINCE the Fleſh of Eels, ſeaſon it with Salt, Pepper, Cloves and Nutmeg; cut the Fleſh of another Eel into Lardoons; then lay one Lair of them on the Skin, and another of the minced Fleſh, continuing ſo to do, till you have made it into the Shape of a Brick of Bread; put the Skin about it, and wrap it up in a Cloth, and ſtew it in half Water and half red Wine; ſeaſon it with Pepper, Salt, Cloves and Bay Leaf; let it cool in its own Liquor, and when you are going to ſend it to Table, cut it in Slices.

To roast a large Eel.

WASH it in Salt and Water, cut off the Head, and flea off the Skin a little below the Vent; gut it, wipe it clean with a Cloth, and give it three or four Scores with a Knife; then shread some Parsley, Thyme, and sweet Marjoram, with an Anchovy, and some scalded Oisters; mix them with Salt and Butter, and put them in the Belly of the Eel, and in the Scores; then draw the Skin over the Eel again, tye the Skin with a Pack-thread, to keep in the Moisture; fasten it to a Spit, and roast it leisurely, baste it with Water and Salt till the Skin breaks, then baste it with Butter; make your Sauce of beaten Butter and white Wine, with three or four Anchovies chopped in it.

To bake Tench.

WHEN they are well cleaned, lay them in a Pan with Gravy, white Wine, and some Mushrooms, Anchovies, and three or four Shalots, some Pepper, Cloves, Mace, Salt and Lemon-peel, with a Bunch of sweet Herbs; lay some Butter all over the Fish, then cover them very close, and bake them an Hour; then pour off the Liquor, and strain it, only preserving the Mushrooms; then add to it a Spoonful of Lemon Juice, and thicken your Sauce with the Yolks of three Eggs, mix it by Degrees with the Sauce, lay your Fish in a hot Dish, and pour the Sauce over them.

To roast Tench.

HAVING cleaned it well from the Slime, make a Hole as near the Gills as you can, stuff the Belly as full of sweet Herbs as you can, then tye it to the Spit, and roast it; mix Butter with Vinegar and Salt, and baste it often; give it what Fish Sauce you please.

To fry Tench.

SLIT them down the Back, drudge them with Flour and Salt, then fry them; make the Sauce of Gravy

Mush-

Mushrooms, Artichoke Bottoms, Truffles, Anchovies and Capers, all chopped small, and well stewed; the Juice of a Lemon, and some Fish Cullis, or a Piece of Butter worked in Flour; boil it very well; send your Fish with Parsley on it, the Sauce in a Bowl.

To crimp Scate.

CUT the Fish the cross Way into ten Pieces, Inch broad, ten long, more or less, according to the Size of the Fish, then boil it quick in Salt and Water; put it dry on a Dish, and strew on it green Parsley; if it is to be eaten hot, put in one Cup Butter and Mustard, and, in another, Butter and Anchovy; send Oil and Vinegar to Table with it.

Flounders with Sorrel.

CUT three Scores on one Side of them, and lay them in a Pan with as much Water as will cover them, with a little Vinegar and Salt, boil them quick; then boil four Handfuls of Sorrel picked, and chop it very small; put it over the Fish, and pour half a Pound of melted Butter over it; drain the Fish very well.

To boil Flounders or Plaice.

PUT Salt, whole Pepper, white Wine, Vinegar, and a Bunch of sweet Herbs into your Water; let it boil apace before you put in your Fish; let them boil till they swim, then take them up and drain them; take a little of the Liquor, put in it some Butter work'd in Flour, two Anchovies and some Capers; beat it up thick on the Fire, then pour it in a Sauce Boat; put Parsley and sliced Lemon on the Fish.

To broil Flounders or Plaice.

SPLIT them, put Parsley and green Onions cut in a Stew-pan, with Pepper, Salt, and a Lump of Butter; put in your Plaice or Flounders, and turn them two or three Times, to make them get a Taste, with-

out

out putting them over the Fire; then strew them with Crumbs of Bread, and put them a broiling; when done, you may serve them up with any Sauce you please.

To stew Plaice or Flounders.

CUT them into, and place them in the Stew-pan, with as much Water as will cover them, put in a Blade of Mace, Salt, Lemon-peel, and a Spoonful of Lemon Juice, mix'd with Crumbs of Bread, Pepper, Nutmeg, Thyme, Parsley and Onion shred small; then stew them on a slow Fire, lay the Fish in the Dish, and pour it on them; or you may put them in the Pan with white Wine, Truffles, Mushrooms, Parsley, Thyme, Chives, the Melts, and a little Butter and Flour, stir and turn them, but don't break them, put in the Yolks of two Eggs, well beaten; to fry them, only drudge them with Flour, and fry them brown, and put fried Parsley over them when brandered; the Sauce is melted Butter and Vinegar.

To dress Cabbolow.

BOIL it in boiling Water till it fleaks, put it on the Dish, and strew a good deal of hard Eggs, chopped fine over it, or you may leave the Fish in Heaps, and the chopped Eggs in Heaps; you may dress any salt Fish the same Way: If it is too dry, steep it before it is boiled, and send a Bowl of Butter and Mustard to Table with it.

To pot Salmon, Trouts or Eels.

CUT off the Heads and Fins, scrape and wipe them very clean, cut them in middling Pieces, season them very well with Pepper, Cloves, Mace and Salt, put them in a Can, and put a good deal of Butter about them, cover them with coarse Dough, made of Meal; put them in a slow Oven: The Salmon will take an Hour baking, the rest but half an Hour; when they come out of the Oven, take them out of the Can, and let them drain well from the Liquor, and let both cool; then take all the Butter off the Can, and clari-

fy

fy it with more Butter to cover your Fiſh, put them in ſmall Pots, and pour the clarified Butter over it; you may ſend them to Table in the ſmall Pots: If you find they don't come eaſy from the Bones, put them a while longer in the Oven.

To pot Lobſters or Scollops.

LET your Lobſters be as whole as you can, take them out of the Shell, and your Scollops quite whole, put them in different Pots, and the leſs the Pots are, the better; ſeaſon them with Pepper, Salt, Cloves and Mace, put a good deal of Butter on them, put them in a ſlow Oven, and cover them; half an Hour bakes them, as they were boiled before; when cold, put clarified Butter over them.

To fricaſey Oiſters, Cockles or Muſſels.

PICK them very clean, and ſtrain a little of their own Liquor on them, with Crumbs of Bread, and a Piece of Butter work'd in Flour; ſeaſon them with Pepper and Mace, a little Salt and Nutmeg, the Grate of a Lemon, a little white Wine, and the Juice of a Lemon; don't put too much Flour among the Butter.

To butter Crabs or Lobſters.

PICK all the Fiſh out of the Shell, put it in a Sauce-pan with Crumbs of Bread, Nutmeg, a very little white Wine, ſtir it about, and when hot, put it in the Shells, and ſome Crumbs of Bread on it, brown it before the Fire, and put the Juice of a Lemon in it, or a Lemon.

To make Caper Salmon.

TAKE out the Chine, ſalt it twelve Hours, then drain it well from the Salt and Blood, take an Ounce of Salt-petre, and an Ounce of Peter-ſalt, and half a Pound of Bay Salt; rub it very well for ſix Days with this, then hang it up to dry by a ſlow Fire.

To keep Salmon in Pickle for a Year.

CUT off the Fins, and chine it, salt it for twenty Hours on a Board, boil a Pickle of Salt and Water, that will bear an Egg, as much as you think will cover the Salmon; when your Pickle is almost boiled, put in it an Ounce of Salt-petre, and an Ounce of Peter-salt, a Pound of Bay Salt, skim it well, and when it is cold, pour it from the Bottom, then put your Salmon in it; a Lime Can is best to keep it in; cut the Salmon in Pieces, as much as you think proper to boil at once.

To stew Haddocks or Whitings.

PUT them in the Pan, with a little Water, Pepper, Salt, Mace, chopped Pasley, Lemon-peel and Onion, a good Piece of Butter worked in Flour; let them boil on a quick Fire. When you think they are enough, put in a little Wine, then take out the Fish, and thicken the Sauce with the Yolks of three Eggs well beaten; take Care it does not curdle: When you put Butter and Flour in any thing, stir it till it dissolves; shread the Parsley.

To pot Herrings.

CUT off the Heads and Fins, put them in a Pan; season them with Pepper, Salt and Vinegar: If you put in a little Sherry in them, put the Juice of a Lemon instead of Vinegar: Cover them close, and bake them in a slow Oven: They are to be eaten when cold. Eels may be done the same Way.

To pickle Oisters, Scollops, Cockles or Mussels.

WASH and pick them clean in their own Liquor, then strain the Liquor, put them in it with whole Pepper, Cloves, Mace and Salt; give them two or three Boils, then take them off, and eat them cold: A little of it is good in any Fish Sauce.

To

To scollop Oisters or Lobsters.

SCALD the Oisters, put them in the Scollop Shells, put a little Butter in the Bottom; season them with Nutmeg, the Grate of a Lemon, a very little Pepper, some of their own Liquor, and a little white Wine: Put Crumbs of Bread over them; then put them in a slow Oven. Cut the Lobster in Dice, and do it the same Way. You may do them before the Fire on a Brander.

To stew Eels.

CUT the Tails and Fins if large, skin them; cut them three Inches long: Season them with Pepper, Salt and Cloves; put them in a Stew-pan, with a little Gravy or Water, a Bunch of sweet Herbs, and two Onions: Cover them close, and let them stew on a slow Fire. When the Fish comes easy from the Bone, they are done. Take out your Herbs, and put in Crumbs of Bread, and a little Butter worked in Flour, a Glass of white Wine, and the Squeeze of a Lemon.

To make a Fricasey of Oisters.

PICK your Oisters very clean, put them on the Fire, and give them a Scald, skim them and drain them clear from their own Liquor; strain the Liquor, put it in a Sauce-pan with the Oisters, the Rind of a Lemon, an Onion stuffed with Cloves, a Blade of Mace, a Piece of Butter worked in Flour; when the Rawness is off the Flour they are enough, put Sippets in the Ashet under them: Take out the Onion and Lemon-peel, and put a little white Wine, and the Juice of a Piece of Lemon in them, Pepper and Salt; thicken them with the Yolks of two Eggs.

To make Forc'd-meat for Fish.

CHOP a large Haddock very small, and put as much chopped Sewet as Fish, and as much Bread, and a few chopped Oisters; season it with Pepper and Nut-

meg,

meg, a little ſhred Parſley, Onion, Salt and Lemon-peel; wet it with an Egg or two, ſo roll it in ſmall Balls, flour your Hands as you are rolling them; fry them in Butter a light brown, they will ſerve any Sort of Fiſh.

To fry Soals.

FLEA them, and drudge them with Flour, and get a Pan almoſt full of clarified Butter, or good Drippings of Beef; when it is boiling hot, put in the Soals and fry them a good Brown on both Sides; drain them very well from the Fat, put criſped Parſley and Slices of Orange over them. Or, you may give them a Sauce made thus: Take two Gills of Gravy, the ſame of Claret, an Onion ſtuffed with Cloves, Mace, and a little Salt or Anchovy Liquor; brown ſome Butter and Flour, and ſtir it in by Degrees, with chopped Morels, and Forc'd-meat Balls; you may put fried Oiſters in it, and a little Oiſter Liquor: Send it in a Sauce Boat.

A good Way to dreſs Lobſters.

PARBOIL your Lobſters, break the Shells, pick out all the Meat, cut it ſmall, take the Meat out of the Body, mix it fine with a Spoonful of white Wine, put it in the Stew-pan with the reſt; cut the Tail in long Pieces, put in a Piece of Butter and a Gill of white Wine, ſome Crumbs of Bread, a little Pepper, Salt, Nutmeg, and a Spoonful of Vinegar: Let it ſtew a little, put in a Gill of Gravy; when hot, diſh it.

Lobſters the Italian *Way.*

WHEN your Lobſters are boil'd, take the Meat out of the Tail and Claws, and cut it in Slices; put a little Butter in a Stew-pan, Parſley, Muſhrooms and Truffles cut ſmall, with a little Gravy, and a Glaſs of white Wine; ſeaſon it with Pepper, Salt, Nutmeg, ſweet Herbs, and Rockambole: Let it ſtew ſlowly, put the Meat of the Body and Juice of Lemon in it.

To dress Crabs.

TAKE the Meat out, and cleanse it from the Skins, put it into a Stew-pan, with two Gills of white Wine, some Crumbs of Bread, the Grate of a Lemon, Nutmeg, Pepper and Anchovy; put it on the Fire with a little Butter, stir it with the Yolk of an Egg, so dish it: You may put Claret, instead of white Wine, if you please.

To make Water Sokey.

TAKE some of the smallest Flounders you can get, cut the Fins close, put them in a Stew-pan, and as much Water as will cover them; put Salt and a Bunch of Parsley, boil them till they rise to the Top: Send them to the Table with the Liquor about them; put Parsley and Butter in a Cup.

To stew Trouts.

PUT your Trouts in a Stew-pan, with two or three Gills of white Wine, and a Quarter of a Pound of Butter, Pepper, Salt and Mace, minc'd Parsley, Thyme, and green Onions: Let them all stew a Quarter of an Hour, then mince the Yolks of two Eggs and put them in. Dish them and pour their own Liquor over them.

To souse Trouts.

PUT all Sorts of Spice, and a Faggot of sweet Herbs, in as much Water and Vinegar as will cover the Fish, boil them in it: When they are enough, let them lye in the Pickle till you are for eating them.

To fry Lobsters.

TAKE a boiled Lobster, and take out the Meat as whole as you can, slice it the long Ways, flour it and fry it in clarified Butter; or you may make a Batter of Cream, Eggs, Flour and Salt, dip them in it and fry them: Then beat some Butter up thick, with grated Nutmeg, Claret and Orange Juice. Lay the Lobsters in the Dish, and pour the Sauce on it.

To stew Crabs.

BOIL them, take the Meat out of the Bodies, save the great Claws, mash the Meat that is in the Body, and mix it with Claret, Vinegar, Salt, Nutmeg, and a Piece of Butter: Put them in a Stew-pan with chopped hard Eggs, let them stew a good while, then put them in the Shells. Put them in the Dish with the Claws broiled round them.

To boil a Piece of Sturgeon.

TAKE a Rand of Sturgeon, put a Mutchkin of Vinegar, two Chopins of Water, some Slices of Lemon-peel, Horse-radish, Bay Leaves, whole Pepper, Ginger, Cloves and Salt. The Liquor must boil before you put in the Fish: If it is to be eat hot, make the Sauce either of Oisters, Lobsters or Crabs; if it is to be kept in Pickle to be eaten cold, don't put in Vinegar, but put in a good deal of Salt, and all Sorts of Spices.

To roast a Piece of Sturgeon.

LAY your Sturgeon in Salt and Water six Hours, then spit it, and baste it well for a Quarter of an Hour; then drudge it with grated Bread, Nutmeg, Mace, Pepper, Salt, sweet Herbs, Lemon-peel cut small; continue drudging and basting till it is enough. Make the Sauce of Gravy, Oister Liquor, Lemon-peel, sweet Herbs, Onions, Ketchup, Pepper, Salt, Mace, and some white Wine; strain it off, and put in as much Butter as will thicken it: You may put in either Oisters, Prawns, Lobsters or Crabs.

To fry Sturgeon.

TAKE a Piece of fresh Sturgeon, and cut it in Slices Half an Inch thick; slash it, and fry it in clarified Butter; then take it up and clean the Pan, and put in Claret, Lemon-peel, Nutmeg, Pepper, Salt and Anchovy. Let all stew a while, then put in a Piece of Butter roll'd in Flour and Shalot.

To

To fry Sperlings.

DRY them, and rub them with an Egg, roll them in Crumbs of Bread, Lemon-peel, Parsley, Pepper, Salt, and fry them brown in clarified Butter. Send Parsley and Butter in a Cup.

To stew Sperlings.

PUT them in a Pan, with a little Gravy, white Wine, the Yolks of three or four Eggs minc'd small, a good Piece of Butter, an Onion stuffed with Cloves, a little Pepper and Salt. Let them stew till done; put the Squeeze of a Lemon in it. Send it up hot.

To boil Mackarel.

BOIL them in Salt and Water, with a little Fennel: The Sauce is the Fennel chopped small, with beat Butter, or scalded Gooseberries, with Butter and Sugar.

To pickle Mackarel.

CUT them in Pieces, and season them with Pepper, Salt, Mace and Cloves, rub them with it, and let them lye a while; then fry them in clarified Butter; then put them to drain; and when they are dry, put them in a Can, then boil Vinegar and Spiceries; and when it is cold pour it on them.

To broil Mackarel.

WHEN they are well clean'd, draw them at the Gills; wipe them and stuff them with Crumbs of Bread, the Liver, Parsley, Pepper, Salt, Nutmeg grated, Lemon-peel, Shalot, and wet it with an Egg, then brander them, and when done pour over them beat Butter.

To fry Maids.

SKIN them, and put them in Salt and Water, let them lye a while, then dry them with a Cloth; flour them, beat six Eggs, with a little Flour, Salt, Ginger, Nutmeg, Parsley shred small, a little white Wine, beat it it up pretty thick; have a Pan with Beef Drippings, or clarified Butter boiling hot; dip your Maids in the Batter, and fry them brown. Let the Sauce be Butter, Vinegar, the Livers of the Fish, and Nutmeg beaten together; put fried Parsley over them, and the Sauce in a Boat.

To boil Gurnets.

STUFF the Bellies with Bread Forc'd-meat, and boil them in Salt and Water; drain them well: The Sauce is beat Butter, Nutmeg, Lemon Juice, Shrimps, or Cockles, and a boiled Anchovy: When you broil them, you may give them the same Sauce, with a little Gravy in it.

To fry Whitings.

GUT them, and wipe them clean with a Cloth, and turn their Tails into their Mouths; make a Batter of Eggs, Flour, and a little Salt; dip them in it, and strew on them Crumbs of Bread; then fry them a light brown. The Sauce is beat Butter and Anchovies, or Parsley and Butter.

To stew Scollops.

BOIL them very well in Salt and Water, take them out and stew them in a little of the Liquor, a little white Wine, Mace, Cloves, and a Piece of Butter rolled in Flour, a little Juice of Lemon and some Salt: You may do Cockles or Mussels the same Way; but scald them in their own Liquor.

To make a Collar of Fish.

TAKE a large Eel, skin it, and pick off the Flesh, and beat it in a Marble or wooden Mortar; season it with beaten Mace, Nutmeg, Pepper and Salt, sweet Herbs, Parsley, Lemon-peel and Shalots, all chopped small; beat all well together, with an equal Quantity of Crumbs of Bread; then take

any

any flat Fiſh that will roll, and lay it on the Dreſſer. Take out all the Bones and Fins, and cover your Fiſh with the Forc'd-meat; mix a Couple of raw Eggs with it; then roll it up tight, and open the Skin of the Eel, and bind the Collar with it, ſo that it may be flat Top and Bottom. To ſtand well in the Diſh, butter an Earthen Can, and ſet it in it upright; flour it, and put a Piece of Butter on the Top, and round the Edges. Let it be well baked, but take Care it is not broke; put two Gills of Water and a little Vinegar in the Can; take another Eel cut in Pieces, and put it in a Sauce-pan, with a Bunch of ſweet Herbs, Onion, Truffles, Morels, and a few Muſhrooms; cover it cloſe, ſeaſon it with Cloves, Mace, Pepper and Salt: When well ſtewed, take out the Herbs and Onions, and put in it a Bit of Butter work'd in Flour, a little Ketchup and Lemon Juice. Make ſome of the Forc'd-meat in little Balls, and fry them a light brown; when the Fiſh is enough lay it in the Diſh, ſkim all the Fat off it, and pour the Gravy to your Sauce, let it all boil together till it is pretty thick; then pour it over the Roll, and put in your Balls: Garniſh with Lemon and Pickles.

To ſtew a Pike.

Lard with the Fleſh of an Eel; then put it in a Stew-pan, with ſome brown'd Butter and Flour, a little white Wine, Salt, Pepper, Nutmeg, an Onion ſtuffed with Cloves, Lemon-peel, and ſweet Herbs. Let it ſtew on a gentle Fire; then put to it a Ragoo of Muſhrooms, Oiſters, and the Liquor wherein they are ſtewed. Diſh your Fiſh, pour over it the Ragoo, garniſh it with fried Oiſters, the Rands of Fiſh, Pickles, and Slices of Lemon. When your Fiſh is ſtewing keep it cloſe covered, put a little Verjuice in with the Fiſh.

F CHAP.

CHAP. III.

To pot and make Hams, &c.

To pickle Tongues.

LET your Tongues be very well ſalted, and lye in it two or three Days; then make a Pickle for them: Put a Quarter of Salt-petre, a Quarter of a Pound of Peter-ſalt, three Pounds of Bay Salt, and three of white Salt, in ten Chopins of Water; let it boil two Chopins away: See it be well ſkim'd; and when cold put it on your Tongues, but dry them firſt in a Cloth. This Pickle will ſerve either Pork, Geeſe, or Sheeps Tongues. If you ſee it grows muddy, boil it again, and put none of the Sediment in it. There muſt be a Pound of coarſe brown Sugar in it.

To make Hams or Bacon.

SALT them on a Table, and lay a Weight on them for two or three Days, then to every Ham or Flitch of Bacon, take a Pound of white Salt, a Pound of Bay Salt, two Ounces of Salt-petre, and two of Peter-ſalt, a Quarter of a Pound of brown Sugar; mix them all together, and warm them pretty hot; lay your Hams in a Trough, and rub them very well, turn and rub them every Day for three Weeks; then hang them up to dry by a ſlow Fire, Wood, or Saw-duſt, is the beſt to dry them with.

To boil Hams.

IF they are dry ſoke them in cold Water, and put them in a Pot of cold Water with ſweet Hay about them. A large Ham will take three Hours to boil it, a ſmall one but two, and a middling one two and a Half. If they are to be eaten hot, put Crumbs of Bread upon them;

them; ſtuff the Ham with Cloves if you like it, and put it before the Fire.

To make Mutton Hams.

CUT the hind Quarter of very large fat Mutton like a Ham, then rub it all over with Bay Salt and brown Sugar; let it lye a Day, then put it in the Pickle, made thus: Take a Gallon of Pump Water, two Pounds of Bay Salt, two of white Salt, ſix Ounces of Salt-petre, and four of Peter-ſalt, one Pound of brown Sugar, one Ounce of Salt-prunella; put all in the Water, boil it well, and ſkim it. When cold, put in your Hams, let them lye in it a Fortnight; then hang them up and ſmoke them with Dale-duſt or Shavings; they muſt be dry before you make Uſe of them. You may pickle Bacon Hams the ſame Way, or any Sort of Tongues. When you hang up your Mutton Hams, boil the Pickle and ſkim it, and when cold you may put in Tongues, but ſalt them firſt for three or four Days.

Another Way to make Mutton Hams.

CUT the Mutton Ham-ways, take an Ounce of Salt-petre, a Pound of Salt, a Pound of coarſe Sugar, two Penny-worth of Cochineal, mix them, and rub the Ham very well, lay it with the Skin Side down, and rub it every Day for ſixteen Days, then hang it up to dry. It eats beſt in broil'd Raſhers.

To make Veal Hams.

CUT a Leg of Veal like a Ham; take a Pound of white Salt, a Pound of Bay Salt, two Ounces of Salt-petre, mix them and rub the Ham with it, lay it with the Skin Side down for a Fortnight, rubbing it every Day with the Pickle; hang it up, it will be dry in ſixteen Days. You may boil or roaſt it.

To make Beef Hams.

TAKE a ſmall Leg of Beef, cut it Ham-faſhion; an Ounce of Peter-ſalt and four Ounces of Bay Salt, a Pound of white Salt, a Pound of coarſe Sugar; mix them, and rub the Ham; lay it and all Hams in a Veſſel at full Length that will hold the Brine; turn and rub it every Day for a Month; then hang it to dry, but not in too hot a Place.

To roaſt an Ox or Sheep's Heart.

TAKE all the Blood out of it, and ſtuff it with Forc'd-meat, made thus: Take a Quarter of a Pound of Beef Sewet, mince it ſmall, two Handfuls of Crumbs of Bread, Pepper, Salt and Nutmeg, Lemon-peel, Parſley, Thyme, ſweet Marjoram and Shalots, all ſhred ſmall: Put in a chopped Anchovy, wet it with Eggs, and ſtuff the Heart with Cloves, or lard it if you pleaſe; roll it in buttered Papers, and roaſt it well; it takes a good deal of roaſting; roll ſome of the Stuffing in ſmall Bowls, fry them, and put them in the Diſh with the Heart; take off the Papers, and put Gravy under it.

To roaſt a Haunch of Veniſon.

RUB it over with Butter, and put on it a buttered Paper, make a Paſte of Flour, an Egg and Water, and put it on it, put the buttered Paper over it, tye it on with Pack-thread, and put it to a good Fire; it takes three Hours roaſting if but ſmall, more if large; take off the Paſte and Paper, put Gravy under it, Claret Sauce in a Boat, and Currant Jelly on a Saucer: If you boil a Haunch of Veniſon, let it be well ſalted for ſeven or eight Days, then boil it in a large Pot of boiling Water, ſending it up with Colly-flowers, Savoys or Cabbage.

To roaſt a Shoulder, or any Joint of Veniſon.

LARD it with Bacon, ſeaſon it with Pepper, Salt, Nutmeg and Cloves, lay it four Hours in Steep of white Wine, Lemon Juice and ſweet Herbs, then ſpit

it,

it, roaſt it at a gentle Fire, baſte it with its own Pickle; when roaſted, take what drips from it, and put to it Gravy, and a little Butter work'd in Flour, an Anchovy and Ketchup; boil it, and pour it under the Veniſon, ſo ſerve it up.

To ſtew Veniſon that has been roaſted or baked.

GET a little Gravy, ſome browned Butter and Flour, a Gill of Claret, a Bunch of ſweet Herbs, ſome Shalots, Ketchup, and an Anchovy, ſeaſon it with Pepper and Salt, boil it till it is ſmooth, then cut the Veniſon in thin Slices, and give it but one Scald; take out the Herbs, and ſqueeze in it the Juice of a Lemon, ſo ſerve it up hot.

To ſouſe Veniſon.

BOIL it in Water, Beer and Vinegar, ſkim it; then put in Thyme, Savoury and Bay Leaves, ſeaſon it with Pepper, Salt and Nutmeg.

To ſtew Veniſon.

CUT it in Slices, put it in a Stew-pan with Claret, Sugar, grated Bread, three or four Cloves, and a little Vinegar; let it ſtew for ſome Time, grate in Nutmeg, and ſerve it up; Veniſon may be haricot after the ſame Manner as Mutton is.

Veniſon in Blood.

THE Shoulder, Neck or Breaſt muſt be boned, and laid in Blood; ſeaſon it with Pepper, Salt, Winter Savoury, ſweet Marjoram and Thyme, all ſhred ſmall, with a little Beef Sewet chopped ſmall, and ſtirred on the Fire to be thick; then roll up the Veniſon with the ſet Blood and Herbs, and roaſt, or ſtove it gently in good Broth or Gravy, Claret and Shalots; ſo ſerve it up hot.

To

To dress Venison à la Royale in Blood.

SPIT your Venison, lay it down to the Fire till it is half roasted, then take it off and stew it; make for it a Ragoo of Cucumbers, Sweet-breads and Asparagus.

To recover Venison when it stinks.

TAKE as much Water in a Tub as will cover it, and put in a good deal of Salt, and let it ly three or four Hours; then take it out, and let it ly as long as before, in hot Water and Salt; take it out, and season it with Pepper and Salt, but dry it first; put some fresh Sheeps Blood in the Dish with it; it must be high seasoned; don't use the Bones of the Venison for Gravy, but put good fresh Gravy in it, cover it with Paste; it will eat best cold.

Venison in Avet.

CUT it into Pieces, the Bigness of your Hand, lard it with Bacon, season it with Pepper and Salt, put it in a Stew-pan with Broth, white Wine, a Bunch of Herbs and Lemon-peel; the whole being stewed, thicken your Sauce with Butter and Flour, and put a little Vinegar in it: It is a first Course Dish; serve it up hot.

A Civet of Venison.

BOIL the Breast or Neck, cut it into Cutlets, and when it is almost boiled, brown half a Pound of Butter, and a good Handful of Flour; then add half a Pound of Sugar, and as much Claret as will make it of a good Thickness, then put in the Venison, and give it three or four Boils, so serve it up; put the Juice of Lemon it it.

To keep Venison all the Year.

A Haunch of Venison being parboiled, season it with two Nutmegs, a Spoonful of Pepper, and a good Quantity of Salt; put to it two Spoonfuls of Vinegar, make the Venison full of Holes, and put in your Spice and Vinegar,

Vinegar, then put the Venison in a Pot, with the fat Side down, and cover it with two Pounds of Butter; then cover the Pot with coarse Paste, and bake it; when baked, take off the Paste, and lay a Trencher with a Weight on it, to keep it down till it is cold, then take off the Trencher, and lay the Butter flat all over the Venison, then cover it with Paper, and tye it down; send it to Table turned up Side down in a Dish.

To boil a Haunch of Venison.

SALT it for a Week, then boil it in boiling Water for two Hours and a Half, if large: Send it up with either Collyflowers, white Cabbages, or Savoys, and melted Butter: You may boil any Joint the same Way, but don't salt it so long, or boil it so much.

To broil Venison.

CUT your Venison into Slices about Half an Inch thick; season them with Pepper, Salt, and Crumbs of Bread; broil them over a brisk Fire. Serve them up with Gravy.

To make Venison Sokey.

BOIL the Venison, and make a Paste of the Crumbs of brown Bread, some Sugar, Pepper, Salt, Nutmeg and Orange-peel minc'd small, and as much white Wine as will wet it: Mix all with your Hand, and wrap the Venison in it; set it into the Oven for an Hour; then serve it up with white Wine boiled up with Sugar.

To roast a Fillet of Veal.

MINCE Beef Sewet very small, an Anchovy, Lemon-peel, Thyme, Parsley, sweet Marjoram, and an Onion; season it with Salt, Pepper, Nutmeg and Mace; add grated Bread to it: Mix all together with two Eggs, make Holes in the Veal, and stuff it with the Forc'd-meat; put a buttered Paper over it, that the

Stuffing

Stuffing does not come out. Spit it, and roaſt it well; the Sauce is beat Butter, Gravy and Lemon: Garniſh it with ſliced Lemon, and red Beet Roots pickled.

To roaſt a Shoulder of Veal with farcing Herbs.

PARBOIL it a little, then mince ſome Thyme, Parſley, Winter Savoury and Shalot, very ſmall, and mince ſweet Herbs, chop four hard Eggs, a little Pepper, Salt and Nutmeg; mix all this up with two raw Eggs, and ſtuff your Veal with it, but ſave ſome of it; ſpit your Veal, roaſt it, put your Stuffing in the Dripping-pan, and, when the Meat is near roaſted enough, put to it two Gills of Vinegar and a little Sugar. So ſerve it up.

To ſtew a Knuckle of Veal.

PUT it in the Stew-pot with two Chopins of Water, four Blades of Mace, a little whole Pepper, a Sprig of Thyme, an Onion ſtuffed with Cloves, a Cruſt of Bread; cover it cloſe, make it boil, then let it ſimmer for two Hours; lay it in the Diſh, and pour the Broth over it, take out the Thyme and the Onion; or you may make the Sauce better, by putting in a little Ketchup, Walnut Pickle, Truffles, Morels and Muſhrooms.

To broil a Shoulder of Veal.

HALF roaſt it, then ſlice off the moſt Part of it, and ſave the Gravy, put the ſliced Meat in a Stew-pan, with a little Broth and its own Gravy, a little grated Bread, Oiſter Liquor, Vinegar, ſliced Bacon, a Pound of Sauſages out of their Skins made in Balls, and rolled in Yolks of Eggs, Mace, Nutmeg, Salt, Lemon-peel, and an Onion ſtuffed with Cloves. Let all ſtew half an Hour, then put in a Mutchkin of Oiſters, and ſome ſweet Herbs; then take the Bone of the Veal and broil it, and diſh it: Then put in the Liquor a Piece of Butter work'd in Flour; let it boil, then pour it over

ver your broil'd Meat. Garnish with fried Oisters, Barberries, and sliced Lemon.

To roast a Calf's Head.

GET a Calf's Head with the Skin on, and scald it, and boil it an Hour; when cold lard it with Lemon-peel; spit and roast it; when enough, make a Sauce of Gravy, Ketchup, Oisters, white Wine, Lemon, Forc'd-meat Balls, fried Sweet-breads, Mushrooms, Truffles and Morels; put in a Piece of Butter work'd in Flour; boil all together, and pour over the Head: You may do it skinned, if you please.

A Calf's Head Surprise.

YOU must bone it and not split it, clean it well, and fill up the vacant Place with Forc'd-meat, and make it in the same Form as before: You may put in the Middle a Ragoo, and cover it with Forc'd meat. Rub it with Eggs, and strew over it Crumbs of Bread and sweet Herbs, Lemon-peel shred small; season it with Pepper, Salt and Nutmeg; bake it, and put a savoury Sauce under it. Blanch the Tongue, and let it hang out of the Mouth.

To boil a Calf's Head.

BOIL and bone it, then have in Readiness the Palate boil'd tender, Yolks of hard Eggs, Oisters scalded, and Forc'd-meat; season it with Pepper, Salt and Nutmeg: Stuff all in the Head, tie it in a Cloth, boil it three Hours, put Gravy under it, garnish it with Bacon.

Beef à la Daube.

GET a Buttock of Beef, lard it, and force it with Forc'd-meat, then pass it off brown; put in some Broth and a Faggot of sweet Herbs, season it with Pepper, Salt, Cloves, Mace; stove it four Hours very tender, and make a Ragoo of Morels, Truffles, Mushrooms, Artichoke Bottoms, Sweet-breads and Palates, white

Wine and Lemon Juice. Garnish with Petty-Patees and Pickles.

To make Escarlot Beef.

TAKE a Brisket of Beef, half a Pound of coarse Sugar, two Ounces of Bay Salt, one Ounce of Salt-petre, a Pound of common Salt; mix all together, and rub the Beef, put it in an Earthen Pan, and turn it every Day: Let it lie a Fortnight in the Pickle, then boil it with Savoys, or a Pease Pudding. It eats very well cold.

Beef la Vinaigre.

GET a Slice of Beef three Inches thick, most lean, from the Buttock, stew it with a little Water, and a Gill of white Wine; season it with Pepper, Salt, Cloves, a Faggot of sweet Herbs, and a Bay Leaf: Let it boil till it is very tender; then set it a cooling; and when cold serve it up, with Slices of Lemon and a little Vinegar.

To roast a Tongue and Udder.

BOIL the Tongue till it will blanch, put it in cold Water, it will blanch the better, then lard it with Fat of Bacon an Inch long, and stuff the Udder with Cloves, then spit and roast them, baste them with Butter. Serve them up with Gravy, but send in a Boat Claret boiled thick as a Syrup, with Sugar and Currant Jelly, or a savoury Sauce.

Ox Tongues à la mode.

BOIL and blanch and lard it, then brown it off, and stove it one Hour in good Gravy and Broth; season it with Pepper, Salt, Cloves, and a Faggot of sweet Herbs; put in Morels, Truffles, Mushrooms, Sweet-breads, and Artichoke Bottoms; skim off the Fat, and serve them either hot or cold.

To collar Beef.

TAKE a broad Runner of Beef, bone it, rub it with white Salt and Salt-petre, turn it and rub it every Day

Day for eight Days; then dry it in a Cloth, and ſeaſon it with Pepper, Cloves, and *Jamaica* Pepper; roll it very hard, and put it in a Cloth, bind it with broad Netting, and put it in a Pot of boiling Water; let it boil three Hours, then take it up and hang it by one End, and when it is almoſt cold take it out of the Cloth: It is to be eaten cold; you may ſend it to Table either whole or in Slices. You may collar a Flank the ſame Way, but take off the Skin.

To ſtew a Rump of Beef.

CUT off the large Bone, that it may lye flat in the Stew-pan, ſcore the Inſide, and ſeaſon it with Pepper, Salt, Cloves and Mace; ſhread a little Thyme, Parſley, Winter Savoury, and ſweet Marjoram; put Seaſoning between every Score if you like it; lard it with Bacon, and a Slice of Bacon laid in every Score: Put it in your Stew-pot with a Pint of Water, a little Rockambole or Shalots; let it ſtew on a gentle Fire for two Hours, then turn it, and make a Ragoo of Palates and Eyes, Forc'd-meat Balls, and Kernels, with ſome of the Liquor it is ſtewed in; thicken it with brown'd Butter and Flour: Put in your Ragoo a Half Mutchkin of white Wine, and the Juice of a Lemon, the Grate of a Nutmeg, and Muſhrooms if you have them. You may make a Ragoo for it if you pleaſe the ſame Way, of Carots, Turnips, Artichoke Bottoms, Truffles, Morels, Muſhrooms and Oiſters: You may ſtew any Piece of Beef the ſame Way. Boil your Roots before you put them in your Ragoo.

To make Dutch *Beef.*

TAKE ſix Pound of a Buttock of Beef, without Bones, rub it all over with five Ounces of coarſe Sugar; let it lye two Days, then wipe it, and take a Mutchkin of white Salt, two Ounces of Salt-petre, and three of Peter-ſalt; dry all before the Fire, and rub it well into the Beef; then put it in a brown glazed Pan that

that will hold the Beef, and turn it, and rub it every Day for three Weeks: Then put it in a Canvas Bag, and hang it up in any Place where it will dry gradually; turn it often that the Brine does not settle. When dry boil it, and you may either slice or scrape it when it goes to Table.

Beef Steaks with Oister Sauce.

CUT your Steaks off any tender Part of the Beef, flat them with your Chopping-knife, and put them on a hot clean Brander, on a clear quick Fire, turning them often, that the Gravy does not run out, have your Sauce ready, make it thus: Scald your Oisters, and wash them clean in their own Liquor, then strain the Liquor into a Sauce-pan, put to it a Piece of Butter work'd in Flour, two or three Shalots, pounded Pepper, Cloves and Nutmeg, salt it to your Taste; put a Glass of white Wine, and the Rind and Juice of a Lemon in it: So pour it on your Ashet of Steaks boiling hot. Garnish them with Pickles.

To make hung Beef.

TAKE a Surloin of fat Beef, salt it well with white and Bay Salt, Salt-petre, and brown Sugar; let it lye in it for a Fortnight, turning and rubbing it every two Days; then hang it to dry; it eats well either in Rashers, or with Fowls and Greens, but it must not be cut till it is thorough dry.

To boil a Rump of Beef the French *Way.*

BOIL it for Half an Hour, take it up in a deep Dish, cut Gashes in the Side to let out the Gravy, then put Pepper and Salt in every Gash; then fill the Dish with Claret, and some Blades of Mace, set it on a Chaffing Dish of Coals, and cover it close, and let it stew an Hour and a Half; Turn it often, take off all the Fat, put in a Handful of Capers, five Onions, and six hard Lettices, slice them both, put in a Spoonful of Verjuice;

Juice; boil all till the Meat is tender. So serve it up on Sippets.

To stew a Rump of Beef.

BOIL it till it is half enough; take it up and peel off the Skin; then take Pepper, Salt, Mace and Nutmeg, Parsley, sweet Marjoram, Savoury and Thyme shred, stuff them in large Holes thro' the Fat, and lay all the rest of the Seasoning over the Top, and lay it all over with Eggs to bind it; put the Gravy that comes out, with a Mutchkin of Claret, and a Gill of Vinegar, in a deep Pan with the Liquor, you may fill it to the Top. Cover it, and bake it four Hours; then put it in a Dish, and pour the Liquor over it.

To grillard a Breast of Mutton.

HALF boil a Breast of Mutton, score it in Dice, then rub it over with an Egg; take Crumbs of Bread, Pepper, Salt, Thyme, sweeet Marjoram, Chives and Parsley; mix all together, and lay it on it, then broil it gently for Sauce; take Butter, Gravy, Capers, Shalot and Cucumbers, all shred small; garnish it with pickled Onions, red Cabbage and Kidney Beans.

To make Mutton Cutlets.

CUT a Neck of Mutton in single Bones, flat them with the Chopping-knife, season them with Pepper and Salt, rub them with Eggs, and lay all over them Forc'd-meat; make it thus: Chop a little of the lean Mutton, with twice as much Sewet, as much Crumbs of Bread as Mutton, Pepper, Salt, the Grate of a Lemon, Parsley, Thyme and Shalot; chop all very small, and mix them up; wet them with Eggs, roll your Cutlets in buttered Papers, and broil them on a clear Fire: They will take a Quarter of an Hour: When done, take them out of the Papers; the Sauces must be Butter and Gravy, Lemon and Ketchup: You may do Veal the same Way, but it takes longer broiling; garnish them with Pickles; if Veal, with Lemon, Muſhrooms, and Beet Roots.

To roaſt a Collar of Mutton.

BONE a Breaſt of Mutton, and rub it with Eggs; lay all over it Forc'd-meat, made as above, roll it up very tight, and bind it cloſs: You may tye it on a Spit, or do it in the Oven; make a Haſh to put under it; cut your Mutton in thin Bits, brown a little Butter and Flour, put in a little Gravy, put a Bunch of ſweet Herbs, the Rind of Lemon, and two Onions ſtuffed with Cloves, Pepper and Salt, boil it well; then put in your Haſh with Muſhrooms, Cucumbers, and Kidney Beans, mince it, but not ſmall: Don't let your Mutton boil, but give it a Scald or two; it muſt be roaſted before you cut it; put it on the Diſh, and the Collar over it; take off the Binding, and throw out the Onions and Herbs: Put Lemon Juice in the Haſh. Garniſh with Pickles.

To roaſt a Leg of Mutton with Oiſters.

TAKE ſome Crumbs of Bread, a little Beef Sewet, ſome hard Eggs, an Onion, three Anchovies, Thyme, and Winter Savoury, twelve Oiſters, Lemon-peel and Parſley, mince them ſmall; ſeaſon it with Pepper, Salt and Nutmeg; mix all theſe together, and wet them with raw Eggs, ſtuff the Mutton under the Skin in the thickeſt Place, and half roaſt it; cut off ſome of the Under-ſide of the fleſhy End in little Bits, put them in a Sauce-pan, with a Mutchkin of Oiſters and their Liquor, ſeaſon them with Mace and Salt; put in a good Piece of Butter in Flour; and when the Mutton is done, diſh it, and pour the Sauce round it.

A Shoulder of Mutton in Epigramme.

TAKE a Shoulder of Mutton, half roaſt it, and take off the Skin as neatly as you can, the Thickneſs of a Crown, leaving the Shank-bone to it; then cut the

the Meat in thin Slices, the Bignefs of a Shilling; put it into good Gravy with a Piece of Butter, fome grated Bread, Pepper, Salt and Nutmeg, an Onion, Anchovy, and Pickles fhred; rub the Skin over with an Egg, and ftrew it with Crumbs of Bread, Pepper, Salt, Chives and fweet Herbs, fhred fmall; brander it, but don't let the Hafh boil much; difh the Hafh, and put on it the broiled Bone and Skin; you muft not cut them afunder.

Carbonaded Mutton.

CUT a Joint of Mutton in Steaks, and fry them; then ftew them in good Broth, with Crumbs of Bread, a Bunch of fweet Herbs, Mufhrooms, Salt, Pepper and an Onion ftuffed with Cloves; take out the Herbs and Onion before you fend it up.

To boil Sheeps Tongues with Oifters.

BOIL fix Sheeps Tongues in Water and Salt till they are tendr; peel off the Skin, cut them in thin Slices, put them in a Stew Pan with a Chopin of Oifters, a little Claret, Cloves and Mace; fet them a ftewing, then put in fome Butter, and the Yolks of three Eggs well beaten, fhake them well; don't put in the Eggs till you are going to difh them. You muft not let the Eggs boil in them, but be fcalding hot.

To roaft a Calf's Head with Oifters.

CUT the Head as for boiling, take out the Brains and the Tongue, parboil them, blanch the Tongue, and minch them with a little Sage, Beef-fewet and Oifters, with Yolks of Eggs and Crumbs of Bread, Pepper, Salt, Nutmeg, grated Lemon-peel; parboil and dry the Head, fill the Skull with thefe Ingredients, then ftuff it with Oifters, and faften it to the Spit; as it roafts preferve the Gravy, put to it a Glafs of white Wine, Salt, Nutmeg, Lemon-peel and Shalot, a Piece of Butter work'd in Flour, fome Oifters, and

a

a little Lemon-juice, beat it up thick. When the Head is done, dish it, and pour the Sauce about it.

To dress Calves Feet.

BOIL them tender, slit them in the Middle, put them in a Stew-pan with a Gill of Grvay, a Piece of Butter, a little Onion, Parsley chopped small, Pepper and Salt, a Spoonful of Vinegar; stew them all together, so dish them. You may make them sweet, and put Currants and white Wine in them; thicken them with the Yolks of two Eggs.

Cakes of Beef to be fried or brandered.

CHOP some of the tenderest Part of the Beef very small, and pound it as much as for Sausages, mix Half the Quantity of Beef-sewet with it; season it with Pepper and Salt, you may put Onions and Parsley in them, wet them with an Egg, make them in Cakes, and fry them in their own Gravy, or brander them on Papers.

To force the Inside of a Surloin of Beef.

LIFT up the Fat carefully, cut out the Meat to the Bone, and chop it small; cut a Pound of Sewet fine, and as many Crumbs of Bread, a very little Parsley, Lemon-peel, and two Shalots; season it with Pepper, Salt and Nutmeg, mix all together with a Glass of Claret and raw Eggs; then put it in the same Place, and skewer the Fat over it. Paper it, and don't take off the Paper before you dish it. You may put Gravy or Claret to it. Spit the Meat before you put in the Forc'd-meat.

A Neat's Tongue the Polish *Way.*

BLANCH off the Skin and boil it, cut it in two, but not quite off; stick it with Slices of preserved Lemon, and Bits of Cinnamon; then put a Bit of Sugar, a Glass of white Wine, and a little Gravy: Then let the Tongue stew a while, and dish it with the Sauce about it.

To fry a Neat's Tongue.

BOIL and blanch it, then cut it in thin Slices, season it with Nutmeg, Cinnamon and Sugar, dip them in the Yolks of Eggs, put some Butter and a little Vinegar in a Pan, and when it is boiling hot, drop in the Tongue and Eggs by Spoonfuls; when they are done dish them. The Sauce is beat Butter, white Wine and Sugar.

To stew a Neat's Tongue whole.

PUT a raw fresh Tongue in a Stew-pan with good Broth, white Wine, Pepper, Salt, Cloves, Mace and Capers, with Slices of Carots and Turnips: Set this over a gentle Fire, and let them stew two Hours, then take up the Tongue and blanch it, and put some Marrow to it, and let it have a Boil or two, and dish it on Sippets, and pour all over it.

To bake Ox-cheeks.

LET them lye in Water all Night, then bone them and stuff them with Cloves; season them with Pepper, Salt and Mace; put them in a Pan, one Cheek laid close upon the other: Put Bay Leaves on them and a Chopin of Claret, cover the Pan close and bake them well. When they are baked pour off the Fat, and mix it with melted Butter, and pour over the Cheeks. They are to be eaten cold with Mustard and Sugar; the Gravy is to be all poured from it before you put the Butter on.

To roast a Leg of Mutton with Cockles.

STUFF it all over with Cockles and roast it. Put Gravy under it.

To pot Beef.

TAKE a Buttock of Beef, and cut off some thin Slices, and strew on it a little Salt-petre; let it lye four days in it, turning it every Day; then put it in a Can with sweet Butter, or sweet Sewet shred small: Cover it with a coarse Paste made of Meal, and bake it in a hot Oven for three Hours; then take it out, and take all the Greaſe and Gravy from it; when it is cold ſtring it and pound it fine; then ſeaſon it with Pepper, Salt, Cloves, and Nutmeg, then draw ſome ſweet Butter to Oil, and ſkim it, and pour it from the Bottom; to every two Pound of your pounded Meat put a Pound of your oiled Butter, and work it up well together, put it in ſmall white Patees; and, when cold, melt ſome Butter, and pour it on them. You may pot Veniſon the ſame Way.

To make Beef Ollops.

CUT thin Slices of Beef where it is tender, and beat it well with your Rolling-pin; then ſeaſon it with Pepper, Salt, Cloves, Mace and ſweet Herbs, and Lemon-peel very fine; ſeaſon it with Spice as above: Lay a Lair of this all over your Ollops, and roll them up tight; put them in a Can with a little Butter, cover them cloſs and bake them; when they are done, take them out in Slices, and put them on a Diſh, pour on them ſome of their own Gravy, with a little white Wine and the Juice of a Lemon: Don't make it ſour, you may thicken it with a little Butter and Flour, grate Nutmeg in it.

To make Veal Collops.

TAKE a hind Quarter of Veal, and cut the thick Part in very thin Slices, beat them with a Rolling-pin, ſeaſon them with pounded Mace, Cloves, Pepper, and the Grate of a Lemon, then fry them a light brown in ſweet Butter; when they are fried, get ſome good brown Gravy, and thicken it with a little Butter and Flour, boil it with an Anchovy, and a whole Onion, a little Ketchup, and the Juice of half a Lemon: when boil'd put in your Collops, and give them one Boil; if they are not ſeaſon'd enough, put in more of that you ſeaſon'd your Collops with; put Forc'd-meat and an

Anchovy,

Anchovy, and a little Salt. You may put Muſhrooms in them and Oiſters, but ſcald them firſt.

To make Forc'd-meat Balls.

CHOP ſome of the tendereſt Part of Veal or Mutton, very fine, with an equal Quantity of Beef or Mutton Sewet; ſeaſon it with Pepper, Salt, Nutmeg, Cloves, and the Grate of a Lemon, and a little ſweet Herbs; wet it with two Eggs, and work it together with your Hand, make it in ſmall Balls, and fry it in ſweet Butter: Flour your Hands when you roll them.

Another Sort of Forc'd-meat Balls.

CRUMB a Penny Loaf, and add to it eight Ounces of Butter, or Beef Sewet, minc'd very fine, Lemon-peel, Parſley, and a Bit of Onion ſhred fine; ſeaſon it with Pepper, Salt, Nutmeg, wet it with two Eggs, roll it in your Hands to a Paſte, then make it in ſmall Balls the Bigneſs of a Nutmeg; fry them in Butter.

Another Sort of Forc'd-meat Balls.

CHOP an equal Quantity of any tender Meat, with Beef or Mutton-ſewet, and the ſame Quantity of Crumbs of Bread, with Lemon-peel, Parſley and Onion ſhred ſmall; ſeaſon it with Pepper, Salt, Nutmeg and Cloves: Wet it with Eggs, and work it up together, then roll it in ſmall Balls. Fry them in Butter.

To make Veal Fricandos.

CUT a Neck of Veal in Chops, letting two Bones be together; put them in a Stew-pan with a little Water, Lemon-peel, Onions, Pepper, Salt, Mace and Anchovy, and a little ſweet Herbs tied in a Bunch, let it ſtew on a ſlow Fire till the Head is boil'd; then take out your Herbs, Lemon-peel and Onions, and thicken it with Butter work'd in Flour, put a little white Wine and the Juice of a Lemon in it, and Muſhrooms if you

have

have them, and ſome boil'd Artichoke Bottoms cut in Dice.

To force a Leg of Mutton or Lamb.

CUT all the Meat out, but don't break the Skin, to every Pound of Meat put Half a Pound of Beef or Mutton Sewet, chop them very fine, ſhread ſweet Herbs, Lemon-peel and Shalots, mix them with it; ſeaſon it with Pepper, Salt, Cloves and Nutmeg, wet it with two Eggs, mix all together and fill the Skin; ſpit it, and roll about it a well buttered Paper: Tye it cloſs that the Stuffing does not come out, it will take a good while to roaſt it. Put Gravy in the Diſh with it, and a Ragoo of Palates and Sweet-breads: Fry the Loin, and lay it round it.

To make a Mutton or Lamb Haſh.

HALF roaſt either a Shoulder or Jiggit of Mutton or Lamb, cut it in thin Slices; ſave the Gravy; put it in your Pan with a little Butter work'd in Flour, ſome Pickles, Pepper, Salt, Ketchup, Onions, and the Rind of a Lemon cut ſmall; if it is too thick, put in a little Water: Two or three Boils does it.

To make minc'd Collops.

TAKE any Part of the Beef that is tender, and mince it ſmall, to every Pound of it put a Quarter of a Pound of Sewet minc'd very fine, put it in a Toſs-pan, with a little Gravy or Water, and ſome Onions ſhred ſmall; ſeaſon it with Pepper, Salt and Cloves: Let it ſtew on a ſlow Fire till it is tender, then work a very ſmall Bit of Butter in Flour, and give it a Boil in it; ſo ſerve it up. You may cut Pickles in it if you pleaſe.

To make Beef Collops.

CUT your Collops broad, and very thin, flat them with your Chopping-Knife, flour them, and fry them a light brown: Make your Sauce of Gravy, a little Butter work'd in Flour, and a little Ketchup; ſeaſon it with

with Pepper, Salt, Mace and Onions: When boil'd put in your Collops, and Pickles with them. You do either Lamb or Mutton the ſame Way. Don't boil your Meat in the Sauce, but pour it over them. You may brander them, and pour the ſame Sauce with Oiſters on them.

Entry of Sheeps Trotters forced.

SCALD the Trotters, and let them ſtew in a little Water well ſeaſoned; take them up when the Bones will come out, ſtretch them on a Table, put Forc'd-meat in them, and roll them up one by one; place them in a Diſh, and moiſten them with a little Butter; ſtrew on them Crumbs of Bread, Pepper, Salt and ſweet Herbs; put them in the Oven; when brown, diſh them, and put a Ragoo Sauce on them.

Veal Olives.

TAKE ten or twelve thin Veal Collops, rub them over with an Egg; then lay on them Forc'd-meat, and roll them up, roaſt or bake them: When done, pour over them a Ragoo of Sweet-breads. Garniſh the Diſh with Oranges.

Another Way.

TAKE the Fleſh of a Fillet of Veal, and half the Quantity of Beef Sewet chopped very ſmall; add to it Muſhrooms, Oiſters, and two Anchovies, chop them all ſmall; ſeaſon them with a little Thyme, ſweet Marjoram, Parſley, Lemon-peel, all ſhred ſmall; Pepper, Salt, Nutmeg and Mace; then take the Veal Caul, and lay it all over with the Forc'd-meat: You may roll it in two or three Collars; roaſt or bake it; when done, cut it in Slices, and ſerve it up with ſtrong Gravy.

To stuff a Rump or Round of Beef.

CHOP two Handfuls of Parsley very small, and one of Beef Shewet shred small; mix them and Pepper and Salt together, make Holes with a Knife in the Beef, and stuff them full of it: The Beef is to ly salt four Days before it is stuffed; boil it tender: You may eat it either hot or cold.

White Scots *Collops.*

CUT the Veal into thin Slices, beat them with the Rolling-pin: You may lard them if you please; season them with Pepper, Salt, Cloves, Mace, Lemon-peel, and grated Bread, dipping them first in Eggs; stew the Knuckle well, with a Bunch of sweet Herbs, two Anchovies, Cloves, Mace, Pepper and Salt; strain it, and when you are going to send it up, thicken it with a Bit of Butter work'd in Flour; give it two or three Boils, then put into it the Yolks of three Eggs well beaten, a Glass of white Wine, and the Juice of a Lemon, and give it a good Heat on the Fire, but don't let it boil, stirring it all the while. Your Collops being fried, but not brown, lay them in the Dish, and pour your Sauce over them. Garnish it with Mushrooms and Oisters; don't make it too sour.

To stew a Knuckle of Veal.

LAY at the Bottom of your Pot four long wooden Skewers, wash the Veal, and lay it in the Pot with three Blades of Mace, some whole Pepper, a Sprig of Thyme, a small Onion, a Crust of Bread, and two Quarts of Water; cover it close, and let it come to the Boil, then let it only simmer for two Hours; then take it up, and strain the Broth over it; put young Pease or Asparagus in it.

Lamb with Rice.

HALF roast a fore Quarter of Lamb, put a Pound of Rice into two Quarts of good Broth, three Blades of of Mace, Salt and Nutmeg: let it ſtew an Hour; take it off, and put in the Yolks of four Eggs, and a Pound of Butter; then put in the Lamb in Joints in a Diſh, with the Rice over it, waſh it with Eggs, and bake it half an Hour: You may do Hens or Chickens the ſame Way, but leave them whole.

To make a Calf's Head Haſh.

HALF boil your Head, and cut the one Half in thin Slices; put it in your Pan with Gravy, a Bunch of ſweet Herbs, the Rind of a Lemon, a whole Onion, and an Anchovy; ſeaſon it with Pepper, Salt, Mace and Nutmeg. When it is almoſt boiled, thicken it with Butter work'd in Flour; put in a little ſweet Cream: Score the other Half, and ſtrew on it Crumbs of Bread, ſhred Parſley, Lemon-peel, Pepper, Salt and Nutmeg; put it in the Dripping-pan to brown, baſte it with Butter; when done put it in your Diſh, and before you pour your Haſh about it, put in a little white Wine, ſome Lemon Juice and Muſhrooms, if you have them, and Oiſters; you may make it brown without Cream.

To make a Lamb's Head Haſh.

BLANCH and clean your Head very well, half boil it, cut the Haricals in thin Slices, and take a little of the Water it is boiled in, and put your Haſh in it, with an Onion ſtuffed with Cloves, the Rind of a Lemon, Pepper and Salt, a little Ketchup; thicken it with Butter work'd in Flour, take out the Brains, and mix them with Crumbs of Bread, grated Lemon-peel, Nutmeg, Pepper, Salt, and an Egg; then put them in the Head again, and lay it in the Dripping-pan till it is well roaſted, then put it in your Diſh, and pour your Haſh round it. Garniſh all your Haſhes with Lemon, and put a little of the Juice in them.

Another

Another Way to dreſs a Lamb's Head.

HALF boil the Head, cut it through the Scull into Halves, take out the Brains, mince the Haricals ſmall, and the Brains amongſt them, put them in the Stew-pan with a little Gravy, or ſome of the Water that they were boiled in, with a little Butter work'd in Flour, the Grate of a Lemon, Onion and Parſley minced ſmall, a little Ketchup, the Squeeze of a Lemon, Pepper, Salt and Nutmeg; boil all together, put the Head in a Dripping-pan, rub it over with an Egg, and throw on it Crumbs of Bread, ſweet Herbs ſhred ſmall, Pepper, Salt and Nutmeg; baſte it with Butter: When it is done enough, put it on the Diſh with the Haſh about it, fry the Liver in thin Slices, and put it about your Diſh.

To ſtew a Lamb's Head.

PUT the Lamb's Head in your Sauce-pan, with a little good Broth, made of a Neck of Beef; put all the Haricals in but the Liver; when they are enough, put in a good deal of Spinage, a little Parſley, and an Onion; ſeaſon it with Pepper, and Salt, and let it ſtew on a ſlow Fire: You may put in it half a Pound of Prunes, and thicken it with Crumbs of Bread, if you pleaſe.

To dreſs any Sort of Liver.

CUT the Liver in thin Pieces, and rub it all over with Eggs; take Crumbs of Bread, ſweet Herbs, Onions, and Lemon-peel ſhred ſmall, and ſtrew it on it, ſeaſon it with Pepper and Salt: You may either fry, or broil it; make your Sauce of a little Gravy, thickened with Butter work'd in Flour, the Juice of a Lemon, a little Ketchup, and grated Nutmeg.

To roaſt a Ham or Gammon of Bacon.

TAKE off the Skin, and lay it to ſteep in luke warm Water; then lay it in a Pan, pour on it a Mutchkin of Canary, and let it ſteep in it twelve Hours; then ſpit

ſpit it and paper it over the fat Side; pour the Canary it was ſoaked in, into the Driping-pan, and baſte it with it all the while it is roaſting; when it is roaſted enough, pull off the Paper and drudge it well with Crumbs of Bread, and Parſley ſhred fine, brown it well and ſet it to cool. Serve it with green Parſley.

To roaſt Pork without the Skin.

TAKE any Joint of Pork not ſalted, and lay it to the Fire till the Skin may be taken off; then take it up and take off the Skin; then ſalt it and roaſt it, make Sauce for it of Claret, Crumbs of Bread and a little Water; boil all together, put to it ſome Salt, a Piece of Butter, Lemon-juice, or Vinegar; when the Pork is roaſted flour it; then diſh it, and pour the Sauce to it.

To roaſt a Breaſt of Pork.

TAKE a Fore-quarter of Pork and cut off the Knuckle, divide the Neck from the Breaſt, take out all the Bones, rub it well with Salt, ſhred Thyme and Sage ſmall; mix with it Nutmeg, Cloves and Mace; ſtrew them all over the Meat, then roll it up tight with the Fleſh inward; tie it faſt together, ſpit it long-ways and roaſt it; put Gravy and Muſtard under it.

To broil Pork Steaks.

CUT a Loin or Neck of Pork in thin Steaks, ſeaſon them with Salt and Sage ſhred ſmall; lay them on the Brander, then ſeaſon the other Side; let the Sauce be beat Butter, Vinegar and Muſtard.

To dreſs a Pig the French *Way.*

SPIT your Pig, lay it down to the Fire, and let it roaſt till it is thoroughly warm; then take it off the Spit and divide it into twenty Pieces; ſet them to ſtew in white Wine, and ſtrong Broth, ſeaſoned with Nutmeg, Pepper and Salt, two Onions, and two Anchovies cut ſmall, and a little Butter and Vinegar; ſtew them all, and when enough diſh it in the Liquor it was ſtewed in, with ſliced Orange or Lemon.

A Hog's Head Cheeſe Faſhion.

BOIL it till the Bones come out, then ſeaſon it with Pepper, Salt and Cloves; while it is hot put the thin Side of one half, and the thick of the other together; put a Cloth over and under it in a ſmall Broth-diſh, and lay a Weight on it as broad as the Head is, till it is cold; then take it out of the Cloth; you may ſend it whole to the Table, or in Slices. It is to be eaten with Muſtard and Vinegar, and Onion, if you pleaſe.

Pork Brawn.

GET a Fore-quarter of the beſt and firmeſt Pork you can get, cut off the Shank and bone it, ſalt it with a quarter of an Ounce of Salt-petre, and half an Ounce of Petre-ſalt, two Penny worth of Cocheneal; pound them and mix them with a little Salt and brown Sugar; then lay it on a Table with a Weight upon it for four Days; then wipe it dry and roll it up hard, and bind it with broad Tape; put it in boiling Water, and let it boil four Hours, ſtill keeping the Pot full of Water; if it is large, it will take five Hours boiling.

In Imitation of Brawn.

BOIL a Set of Nolts Feet very tender, then take a Piece of Pork, boil it near enough; then put the Fleſh of the Feet in the Middle of the Pork, let both be boiled with Salt; roll it up tight, and put Tapes about it; boil it till it is tender; when cold put it in Souſe.

A Pig in Jelly.

CUT it in Quarters, and lay it in a Stew-pan with two Calves Feet, and the Pig's Feet; put in a Pint of Rheniſh Wine, the Juice of four Lemons, and ſome of the Rind, and one *Engliſh* Quart of Water; ſeaſon it with Nutmeg, Salt and Mace; ſtove it gently for two Hours;

Hours; let it ſtand till cold, then clear the Jelly; and when it is almoſt cold put it on the Pig; you may cut the Pig into any Shape you pleaſe, and pour the Jelly over it.

To dreſs a Loin of Pork with Onions.

PUT a Loin of Pork to roaſt, and put twenty ſmall Onions in the Dripping-pan under the Pork; let the Fat drop on them, when the Pork is nigh enough put the Onions into the Sauce-pan: Let them ſimmer over the Fire a Quarter of an Hour, ſhaking them well, then pour out all the Fat; ſhake in a little Flour, a Spoonful of Vinegar, and two Tea Spoonfuls of Muſtard, give them a Boil. Lay the Pork in the Diſh, and the Onions in a Sauce Boat.

To roaſt a Quarter of young Pig, Lamb Faſhion.

CUT the Pig in Quarters, and take off the Skin, ſcore it in the Middle with a little Blood, roaſt it a light brown, it will eat like Lamb, with Spearmint, Sugar and Vinegar. The other Part of the Pig you may do in Jelly thus: Bone it, and boil it in a ſmall Quantity of Water, with two Penny-worth of Iſinglaſs, whole Pepper, Cloves, Mace, Lemon-peel and Salt: When it is boil'd as tender that you may thruſt a Straw in it, take it out and cut it in Dice, dry it on a Cloth, put a Gill of white Wine, the Juice of a Lemon, and the Whites of two Eggs beaten in the Liquor the Pig was boil'd in, and run it thro' a Jelly Bag. Pleaſe put your Pig that you cut in Dice in a Bowl; and when the Jelly is almoſt cold, pour it over them.

A Pig Rolliand.

BONE it, leaving the Head whole, and rub it over with Eggs; ſeaſon it with Pepper, Salt and Nutmeg, and lay over it ſome Forc'd-meat: Then roll it up, and either roaſt, bake, or ſtove it. You may cut it in four Pieces, and ſend the Head in the Middle: Make the Sauce

Sauce of the Brains and Gravy, Butter, Vinegar, and chopped Sage if you like it.

To make Bologna Sausages.

TAKE a Pound of Bacon, fat and lean together, a Pound of Beef, a Pound of Veal, a Pound of Pork, and a Pound of Beef Sewet, chop them very fine, sweet Herbs and Sage shred very small, and Pepper; and, to season it pretty high, get a large Gut and fill it, boil the Water, and prick the Gut for fear of bursting. Boil it softly an Hour, then lay it on clean Straw to dry; it will keep good a Year in a dry Place.

To fry Sausages with Apples or Potatoes.

TAKE a Pound of Sausages and six Apples or Potatoes, cut them as thick as a Crown, fry them with Sausages a light brown, dish them up hot; stew'd Cabbage, and fried Sausages, or Pease Pudding and Sausages eat very well.

Oister Sausages.

TAKE a Pound of the Lean of a Leg of Mutton, and two Pound of Beef Sewet, shred very fine, three half Mutchkins of Oisters, shread them likewise, mix these with some of the Oister Liquor, Pepper, Salt, Cloves, Mace and three raw Eggs; and make them up as you use them, and fry them in Butter.

Oxford Sausages.

CHOP the Lean of a Leg of Veal or Mutton, with four Pound of Beef Sewet, or Butter; season it with Pepper, Salt, Cloves and Mace; pound them well, with five or six Eggs, and as you use them roll them out long-ways with Flour; when you fry them boil the Butter, and then put in the Sausages; fry them a light brown, this will serve for Forç'd-meat Balls.

A Souse for Brawn.

BOIL Wheat Brawn and Salt very well, then ſtrain it; and, when cold, put in the Brawn: There muſt be a good deal of Salt; new boil it every Fortnight.

To make Sauſages.

TAKE the tendereſt Part of a Leg of Pork, and chop it very ſmall; to every Pound of Fleſh put a Pound of Hog's Fat, or Beef Sewet; when both is finely chopp'd pound them together in a Mortar; ſeaſon them with Salt, Black and *Jamaica* Pepper; they muſt be high ſeaſoned: Let them lye a Day before you put them in the Skins. Let your Skins be very clean, and lye a while in Salt and Water. You may put chopped Sage in them. You may make Mutton the ſame Way; but put no Sage in them.

Pigs Petty-toes.

WHEN the Pig is opened, get the Draught and Feet clean, and boil them; then get a little Gravy, and a Bit of Butter and Flour, an Onion, and two or three Leaves of Sage minc'd ſmall: Cut the Feet in two, and mince the Draught very ſmall; ſeaſon it with Pepper and Salt, boil them together, and ſerve it up; it muſt be a young Pig's Draught.

To roaſt a Pig's Haſlet.

CUT it aſunder, and waſh it well; ſtuff the Heart with Crumbs of Bread, ſhred Sage, Onion, Parſley and ſweet Marjoram, Pepper, Salt and *Jamaica* Pepper; work all this up with a little Butter: Spit them, and ſtrew Crumbs of Bread, and ſome of the ſame Seaſoning all over it, but firſt rub it with an Egg to make it ſtick: Roll the Caul, or a butter'd Paper over it, and tye it faſt; but when you think it done take off the Paper: It takes two Hours to roaſt it. Serve it up with Gravy and Butter, and a little Sage, with a Drop of Vinegar in it.

To

To make a Ragoo of Tripes.

WHEN boiled, cut them in Bits, put them in a Stew-pan with a very little Water, and ſeaſon them with Pepper, Salt, and a Blade of Mace, with ſhred Parſley and Onions; when tenderly ſtewed, put to them a little Cream and Butter, work'd in Flour; ſerve them up with Sippets under them: You may do Cow Heels the ſame Way, but inſtead of Cream, put Muſtard.

To dreſs a large Pig's Feet and Ears.

BOIL them tender in Salt and Water, then cut your Ears in thin Slices, and your Feet in Quarters: When boiled, fry them, and for their Sauce, get melted Butter, Onions, Parſley, Vinegar and Muſtard; boil your Parſley and Onions in your Butter, chopping them firſt.

To make a Ragoo of Muſhrooms.

WASH and dry them, put them in a cloſs covered Sauce-pan, with a little Pepper, Salt, and a Blade of Mace: Put three Spoonfuls of Water in them, put them on a ſlow Fire. They take a great while ſtewing; when tender, chicken them with a little Butter work'd in Flour; and before you ſend them to the Table, put two Spoonfuls of white Wine in them, and half an one of Vinegar or Lemon.

To make a Ragoo of Kidneys.

TAKE them, and cut them in thin Slices, flour them, and fry them in Butter: When enough, pour in a little Gravy or Water, ſeaſon them with Pepper, Salt, and ſhred Onion and Parſley, with a little Vinegar: You may put in a little Ketchup. Give them but three Boils after you ſeaſon them.

To ragoo a Breaſt of Veal.

STUFF it with Forc'd-meat between the Fleſh and the Bones, and lard it with Bacon if you like it, then

then half roast it, and put it in a Stew-pan with Gravy, and stove it till it is enough; then put in Forc'd-meat Balls, Mushrooms, Truffles, Morels and Oisters; season it with Pepper, Salt, Mace and Nutmeg; the Truffles and Morels must be washed and half boiled before you put them in; thicken it with brown'd Butter and Flour, put in a Glass of white Wine and some Lemon Juice.

A Ragoo of Lamb's Stones and Sweet-breads.

BLANCH them in boiling Water, then wipe them dry, and fry them a light brown; then put them in a Stew-pan with some good Gravy, Pepper, Salt, and an Onion, stuffed with Cloves, Mushrooms and Truffles; let them simmer over a gentle Fire; then put in a Piece of Butter rolled in Flour, a little white Wine and Lemon Juice, and boil them, keeping them stirring all the Time to mix the Butter. You may cut them in Slices, and parboil them with blanched Cocks Combs, and not fry them, but toss them with the same Ingredients as before; or you may dip them in Batter, made of a little Ale, Flour, and two Eggs; then fry them, and dish them with nothing but fried Parsley over them, beat Butter, and Juice of Orange in a Cup.

To ragoo a Neck of Veal.

CUT it in Steaks, season it with Pepper, Salt, Cloves and Mace; lard them with Bacon, dip them in Eggs, make up a Sheet of Cap Paper square, and pin the four Corners an Inch high, butter it, set it on the Grid-iron on a slow Fire, put in the Meat, let it do leisurely, keeping it turning and basting; when it is enough, have ready Gravy, Mushrooms, Pickles, Forc'd-meat Balls, and fried Oisters; season it pretty high, lay the Veal in the Dish, and pour the Sauce over it: Put into it white Wine and Lemon Juice.

To ragoo Venison.

LARD a Piece of Venison with Bacon, well seasoned with Pepper and Salt, fry it a light brown, then stew it two Hours in Broth or boiling Water, and some Claret; season it with Pepper, Salt, Nutmeg and Lemon-peel, thicken it with Butter work'd in Flour, put a little Lemon Juice and Capers in it.

A Ragoo of Livers.

GET the Livers of Fowls, Turkeys or Geese, take off the Gall, blanch them; then put them in a Stew-pan, with as much Gravy as will cover them, a Bit of Butter rolled in Flour, Pepper, Salt, Oisters and Ketchup: Let them stew twelve Minutes if large, but six if small. You may put in Crumbs of Bread, and an Onion shred small.

To ragoo a green Goose.

CUT the Goose in two, put it in a Stew-pan with some Butter, sliced Onions, Lemon, Pepper, Cloves and Salt: You may put in a Bunch of sweet Herbs, put it on a slow Fire, stir and turn it often, then make a Ragoo of green Pease, a little Butter, and some good Gravy, Pepper, Salt and Nutmeg; shake in a little Flour; dish your Goose, and pour the Pease on it.

A Ragoo for a Duck à la Braise.

HALF roast the Duck, and carbonade it, then make a Ragoo of Sweet-breads, fat Fowls Livers, Cocks Combs, Mushrooms, if in Season, Asparagus Tops, Artichoke Bottoms and Truffles, all blanched and half boiled; then stew them in Gravy, seasoned with Pepper, Salt, Cloves, and shred Shalots: Put the Duck in the Middle of the Dish, and pour the Ragoo over it.

To ragoo Pigeons.

LARD your Pigeons, cut some of them in two, season them with Salt, Pepper, Cloves and Mace; then brown

brown ſome Butter and Flour, and put in your Pigeons, and brown them; then put in as much Gravy as will cover them, with a Faggot of ſweet Herbs, and let them ſtew on a ſlow Fire; when they are enough ſtewed, take out the Herbs, and put in Shalots, Anchovies, Oiſters and Muſhrooms. You may put about them, when they are diſhed, roaſted Larks, or any ſmall Birds.

A Ragoo of a Calf's Head.

BOIL it, and cut it in long ſmall Pieces, an Inch long, and the Breadth of your Finger; put them in a Stew-pan with a little Gravy, Truffles, Morels, Oiſters, Artichoke Bottoms in Slices, Juice of Lemon, Pepper, Salt and Mace; thicken it with Butter and Flour, boil it, and put white Wine in it.

To make a Ragoo of Onions.

GIVE them a Scald, then drain them, and put Gravy, Pepper and Salt to them: Let them ſimmer on a ſlow Fire a good while, then put to them a Piece of Butter rolled in Flour. They may be eaten with any roaſted or boiled Meat.

A Ragoo of ſtuffed Cucumbers.

TAKE as many Cucumbers as will fill your Diſh, pare them, and ſcoop out the Seeds, blanch them with boiling Water, then put them in cold Water, ſtuff them with Veal, Beef, and Sewet ſhred very ſmall; ſeaſon it with Pepper, Salt, Onions, Lemon-peel and Spice. Thicken it with Butter and Flour.

To fry Tripe Ragoo.

CUT them into ſmall Pieces, dip them in the Yolks of Eggs, and ſtrew on them Crumbs of Bread; fry them of a brown Colour, drain them from the Fat, and ſend them up hot with Butter and Muſtard in a Sauce Boat.

To roast Tripe.

CUT them in ſquare Pieces, make a Ragoo of Forc'd-meat, Crumbs of Bread, Butter, Pepper, Salt and Nutmeg, and the Yolks of two Eggs; ſpread it on the Tripe, roll them up tight, and tye your Rolls on the Spit, flour and baſte it. Serve them with melted Butter and ſliced Orange.

Tripes the Poliſh *Way.*

CUT the Tripes in Pieces, and ſtrew them with Crumbs, Parſley, green Onions, Pepper and Salt; then put into the Stew-pan a Lump of Butter, and when it is brown, put in the Tripes. Let them ſtew till they are of a good Colour; the Sauce is Butter and Lemon.

To boil Tripes.

CUT them in Pieces, and boil them in Salt and Water till they are tender: You may either ſend them in their own Broth, with Onions and Pepper in it, or boil Onions and chop them; then put them in beat Butter, and ſend it in a Boat; ſome Leeks, Parſley and Onions with them.

To make a Ragoo of Palates and Eyes.

WHEN they are cut out of the Ox or Cow's Head, take the Black out of the Eyes; then blanch them in ſcalding Water, and blanch and ſkin the Palates; boil them in Salt and Water, when boiled cut your Palates in thin Slices, and your Eyes in round ones, but let them both be very thin; put them both in your Stew-pan with ſome good Gravy, an Onion ſtuffed with Cloves, a Bunch of ſweet Herbs, Pepper and Salt; ſtew them well, then take out your Herbs and put in a little Ketchup, brown ſome Butter and Flour, then pour all in, keeping it ſtirring all the Time; put a little Lemon Juice or Vinegar in it before you ſerve it up, and Forc'd-meat Balls, Oiſters, and white Wine.

To

To make a Ragoo of Sheeps Tongues and Sweet-breads, or Kernels.

BOIL your Tongues and blanch them; cut them in very thin Slices, and your Kernels in Dice; ſtew them in Gravy with boiled Artichoke Bottoms cut in Quarters; then ſeaſon them with Salt, Pepper, Cloves, and Anchovies; brown your Butter and Flour, put them in it, keeping them ſtirring all the Time; put Lemon Juice, or a very little Vinegar, in it: You may put Truffles and Morels in it, if you pleaſe.

To make a Ragoo of Truffles and Morels.

BOIL them in Water, when boiled ſtrain the Water they are boiled in, and pick and clean them; put them and their own Liquor in a Stew-pan, with Butter, and Flour, Pepper, Salt, Cloves, Anchovies, a whole Onion, and a little Gravy; when they are ſtewed well, put a little white Wine and the Juice of a Lemon in it: Serve them up garniſhed with Forc'd-meat Balls and ſliced Lemon.

To make Brain Cakes.

BOIL and blanch the Calf's Brains, chop ſome of them, and mix them with Crumbs of Bread, Spice, Salt, the Grate of a Lemon, ſweet Herbs ſhred ſmall, and an Egg; then cut in Pieces what you leave, and rub them with an Egg; ſtrew Flour on them; fry them all in a Pan of boiling Liquor; put in the chopped Brains in Spoonfuls, the other in Lumps; garniſh your Heads with theſe.

To make Veal Cutlets.

CUT a neck of Veal in ſingle Bones, and rub them over with Eggs; ſtrew on them grated Bread, Salt, Pepper, Nutmeg, ſhred Parſley, Shalots, and Lemon-peel; mix them with the Crumbs of Bread; brander them on buttered Papers, or you may do them in the Oven on Tin Plates: For your Sauce, get a little Gra-

vy,

vy, a Bit of Butter worked in Flour, a little white Wine; season it with Nutmeg and Salt; put in it a chopped Anchovy, and some Mushrooms, if you have them; garnish your Dish with Pickles and sliced Lemon; put a little Lemon Juice in your Sauce. You may do Mutton or Lamb the same Way.

To mince Fowl, Veal, or Lamb.

WHEN your Fowl or Flesh is half roasted, mince it small; put it in your Stew-pan with a little white Gravy, a Piece of Butter worked in Flour, a Blade of Mace, a little Pepper and Salt, a whole Onion, the Rind of a Lemon, and a little of the Juice, a minced Anchovy, some Mushrooms likeways. Give it but one or two Boils, for fear of making the Meat hard; garnish it with sliced Lemon: Take out the Onion and Lemon-peel before you send it to the Table.

To fry Veal Sweet-breads.

HAVING larded them with Bacon, run a Skewer through them, or a Spit, and roast them till they are brown; then lay them in a Dish, and put Gravy under them.

To farce Veal Sweet-breads.

SCALD the Sweet-breads, and lard them with Bacon, make a Hole in them, and stuff it with good Forc'd-meat, don't make the Hole quite through, then bake them in a Pan; make a Ragoo of Mushrooms, Truffles, Artichoke Bottoms, and Cocks-combs, and Forc'd-meat Balls, and a little good Gravy thicken'd with the Yolks of Eggs; Dish the Sweet-breads, and put a little Juice of Orange, Salt, Mace, and Nutmeg, in the Ragoo; then pour it about them: You may at another Time blanch some Sweet-breads, and cut them in Slices; flour them and fry them, and put beat Butter with Gravy, Nutmeg and Orange about them.

Rolled

Rolled Fricandoes of Veal.

CUT Slices of a Leg of Veal, beat them, lard them, lay them on the Table, the larded Side downwards: Cover them the Thickneſs of a Crown, with Forc'd-meat made of Veal, Beef Sewet or Marrow; ſeaſon it with Pepper, Salt, Nutmeg and Lemon-peel, and a chopped Anchovy: Put Eggs to bind them, roll them up, and you may do them in the Oven, or fry them in a Pan of boiling Fat. You may either put a Ragoo of Sweet-breads and Palates under them, or Gravy, and the Juice of a Lemon. Be ſure to drain the Fat well from them.

To roaſt a Calf's Liver.

LARD your Liver with Bacon faſtened on the Spit, roaſt it at a gentle Fire; baſte it well, and ſerve it up with beat Butter, Gravy, and a little Vinegar. A Calf's Liver brander'd gets the ſame Sauce.

To broil any Sort of Midriffs.

TAKE the largeſt and freſheſt you can get, clean and ſcald them well, ſtuff them with Forc'd-meat, or with Onion, Sage, Pepper and Salt; then ſew them up, and lay them to broil on a moderate Fire; ſerve them up with Gravy, with or without Claret.

CHAP. IV.

To make Pyes and Paſties, &c.

To make a Veniſon Paſty.

BONE and ſeaſon your Veniſon, and let it lye all Night in Seaſoning, boil the Bones that come out of it into good Gravy, put it into the Paſty-pan, with good Puff Paſte about it; it takes a great while to bake it. When

When it comes out of the Oven ſhake it; and if there is not Gravy enough in it, put in more; if it is to be eaten hot, not elſe, Pepper and Salt is the Seaſoning.

To make a Mutton Paſty as good as Veniſon.

BONE your Fore-quarter of Mutton, and put it in Steep in Claret and its own Blood, a Mutchkin of each, let it lye all Night, ſeaſon it with Pepper and Salt; put it in your Diſh with all that it is ſteep'd in about it: Cover it with Puff Paſte, bake it two Hours in a hot Oven. When it comes out of the Oven, ſhake the Diſh; and if it wants Gravy put it in. You may put Blood and Claret in a Veniſon Paſty, if you pleaſe.

To make a Pigeon Pye.

CUT off the Pinions and Feet, draw them, and chop the Liver and Giſſart; mix it with Crumbs of Bread, chopped Parſley, Lemon-peel and Onion work'd up with a Piece of Butter, Pepper and Salt; Seaſon your Pye with Pepper and Salt; put the Stuffing in their Bellies, lay them in the Diſh on their Breaſts, and put a little Butter on them; put the Pinions in the Diſh with them. Cover the Pye with Puff Paſte, ſo bake it in a quick Oven. You may eat it either hot or cold; you may make it without Stuffing if you pleaſe.

To make a Lamb Pye.

CUT your Lamb in middling Pieces, ſeaſon it with Pepper, Salt and Cloves: Put it in your Diſh with hard Yolks of Eggs and Artichoke Bottoms, and a little Gravy or Water. Cover it with Puff Paſte; You may put in Raiſins and Prunes if you pleaſe.

To make a Veal Florentine.

CUT your Veal in ſmall Pieces, ſeaſon it with Pepper, Salt, Cloves and Mace: Put them in your Diſh with Currants and Raiſins, a little Bit of Butter, and the Squeeze of a Lemon, and a Gill of Water. Cover your

your Dish with Puff Paste; and when it comes out of the Oven, have a Caudle of a Gill of Gravy, a Gill of white Wine, a little Nutmeg, thickened with the Yolks of two Eggs, put a litle Sugar in it, and pour it in your Pye. This Caudle will serve for any sweet Pye. Shake the Dish after it is in it.

To make a Chicken Pye.

SCALD your Chickens, and cut them in Quarters, wash them very clean; season them with Pepper, Salt, Cloves and Mace; put them in your Dish with Forc'd-meat Balls, Yolks of hard Eggs, and Artichoke Bottoms. You may make it without this if you please; put a little Butter and Gravy. You may put Fruit in it, if you like it sweet, and make a Caudle for it as above. You may leave the Chickens whole if you please.

To make a Calf's Foot Pye.

BOIL your Feet and mince them with a little Beef or Mutton Sewet, and some Apples shred small, a little Cinnamon and Mace pounded, some Currants well washed and picked; put them all in a Dish with Puff Paste over them, three Quarters of an Hour bakes them: Then have a Caudle of Sherry, Nutmeg and Sugar, thickened with Eggs; the Oven must be no hotter than will bake the Paste. You may make a Chadren Pye the same Way. Put a Gill of Brandy in it.

To make an Eel Pye.

CUT off the Head and Fins, and cut them two Inches long; season them with black and *Jamaica* Pepper, Cloves and Salt. Put them in your Dish, with some Butter and Crumbs of Bread, a little white Wine and Lemon Juice, and Gravy or Water, Half a Mutchkin of either. Cover it with Puff Paste.

To

To make a Goose Pye.

BONE and season it with Pepper and Salt: If your Goose be very fat, bone a Turky, or a Pair of Fowls, and put in with it. You may either raise it or put it in a Dish: It is to be eat cold. It takes a great while to bake it.

To make a Trout Pye.

CUT off the Fins and Heads, season them with black and *Jamaica* Pepper, Mace and Salt, put some Butter in the Bottom of your Dish, then your Trouts; put Gravy and a little Claret in it: Cover it with Puff Paste. When the Paste is baked they are enough. They are good hot or cold. You may bake Carp or Pike the same Way.

To make a Mutton Steak Pye.

CUT a Neck of Mutton in single Bones; season it with black and *Jamaica* Pepper, and Salt, lay them in your Dish with Artichoke Bottoms if you have them, put Gravy or Water in the Dish, and a little chopped Shalot. You may make a Beef Steak Pye the same Way. Put some Oisters in it if you please, and hard Yolks of Eggs.

To make a Lobster or Shrimp Pye.

BOIL your Lobsters and Shrimps, take off the Shells, cut the Lobsters in large Pieces, the Shrimps whole. Put Butter in the Bottom of your Dish; season them with Pepper, Mace, Salt and Nutmeg. Put a little Gravy, Oister Liquor, white Wine, and the Juice of a Lemon in it. You may put both in the Pye if you please. Put Puff Paste on it. A very little bakes it.

To make an Oister Pye.

GET the largest Oisters you can, wash them clean in their own Liquor, and give them a Blanch; get

get alſo half a Dozen Sweet-breads, and cut them in Pieces, put Gravy and Butter in the Diſh; then lay a Lair of each, till your Pye is full, and a Lair of Forc'd-meat Balls; ſeaſon it with Pepper, Salt and Cloves; put a little Oiſter Liquor in it, and ſome Lemon Juice. When baked put in a Caudle of Sherry, the Grate of a Nutmeg, thickened with the Yolks of two Eggs. You may put the Yolks of hard Eggs in it if you like them, and Artichoke Bottoms, or Truffles and Morels.

To make a Skirret Pye.

BOIL and peel your Skirrets, put them in the Diſh, with Butter on the Bottom of it, and a few Crumbs of Bread; cover them almoſt with Cream, Nutmeg and Mace pounded; ſweeten it with Sugar, cover it with Puff Paſte: When it comes out of the Oven, pour in a Caudel made of white Wine, Sugar, and the Grate of a Nutmeg, thickened with the Yolks of two Eggs.

To make minc'd Pies.

BOIL a large Ox Tongue, blanch it, and chop it ſmall, put double the Quantity of Beef Sewet as you have of Tongue, and the double of Fruit, Currants waſhed and picked clean, the Raiſins ſton'd and minc'd, your Sewet minc'd very fine, and half a Dozen Apples minc'd; ſeaſon it with Cloves, Mace, Nutmeg, Lemon-peel, Cinnamon, and a little Sugar and Salt: Put half a Mutchkin of Brandy in it: When you put it in your Pan, put Puff Paſte over and under it: You may put candied Citron, Lemon, and Orange-peel, if you pleaſe.

To make an Apple Pye.

PARE and quarter your Apples, take out the Cores, put Sugar, beat Cinnamon, and the Grate of a Lemon in it, and the Bigneſs of an Egg of Butter: If you pleaſe you may put Marmalade of Orange, or Quince in it: Cover it with Puff Paſte. A Pear Pye is made, the ſame Way, but put the Juice of a Lemon in it; and if your Apples are dry, put Lemon Juice in it: When either is cold, you may pour Cream over them, if you pleaſe.

To make a Beef Steak Pye.

CUT a very tender fat Piece of Beef in thin Slices, beat it with the Rolling-pin, ſeaſon it with Pepper, Salt, and Cloves, ſtrew it with a little chopped Shalot, fill your Diſh, and cover it with Puff Paſte: when it is baked, put in a little Gravy: You may put Oiſters in the Pye, if you pleaſe, and if you do, put in with your Gravy a Glaſs of white Wine. Make a Mutton chopp'd Pye the ſame Way: You may put in it Forc'd-meat, Truffles, Morels, and Artichoke Bottoms, but put them between the Lairs of the Steaks.

To make a Gooſe-berry Pye.

IF your Gooſe-berries are very young, put them in a Stew-pan, and ſtove them with Sugar; when cold, put them in your Diſh, and nick the Paſte that covers them. When the Paſte is baked, they are enough: You may ſend them to the Table as they are, or cream them. If you cream them, cut off the Lid, and pour it on them: If it is thin, boil it, and thicken it with the Yolks of two Eggs, and ſweeten it to your Taſte, but take Care it is not curdled: When it is cold, pour it on, cut the Lid in Pieces, and ſtick it round the Pye.

To make a Hare Pye.

CUT your Hare in Pieces, break the Bones, and ſeaſon it to your Taſte with Pepper, Salt, Cloves, and Mace; lay it in your Diſh with Slices of Butter and Lemon-juice: Cover it with Puff Paſte.

To make a Gibblet Pye.

WHEN your Gibblets are well ſcalded and blanched, break the Bones, and ſeaſon them with Pepper, Salt, Cloves,

Cloves, and Mace; put them to ſtew in as much Water as will cover them; ſet them on a ſlow Fire, and when they are tender ſet them to cool: If you can get the Blood, make a Pudding in the Skin of the Neck thus: Strain the Blood, and put in it a little Sewet ſhred ſmall, ſome Crumbs of Bread, a Gill of Cream, Pepper, Salt, Nutmeg, a little ſweet Herbs ſhred ſmall, and an Onion; lay the Pudding in the Middle of the Diſh, and the Gibblets round it; pour the Broth they were boiled in over them; let them be well ſeaſoned: Cover the Diſh with Puff Paſte.

To make a Lark Pye, or any ſmall Birds.

TAKE the Larks and ſeaſon them with Pepper, Salt, and Mace; ſtuff them with Forc'd-meat, and lay them in the Diſh with Puff Paſte about the Diſh, the Yolks of hard Eggs, Artichoke Bottoms, and a Lair of Forc'd-meat; put ſome Butter over them, and cover it with Puff Paſte: When baked make a Caudle of Gravy, a Glaſs of white Wine, a little Bit of Butter worked in Flour, and the Grate of a Nutmeg; boil it and keep it ſtirring till the Rawneſs is off the Flour; then pour it in the Pye; then ſhake the Pye, and ſend it up hot: You may make it without Forc'd-meat, or Artichoke Bottoms the ſame Way.

To make a Muir-fowl or Partridge Pye.

SEASON them with Pepper, Salt, Cloves, and Mace, very well; take Cabbage Lettice that is whole, and blanch them; lay one between every Fowl; chop a little Shalot, and ſtrew it on the Lettice, with a little of the Seaſoning, as before: Cover the Diſh with Puff Paſte, cut it in the prettieſt Faſhion you can: When it is baked make a Sauce of two Gills of Claret, a little Gravy, an Anchovy, and a little Nutmeg; pour it in the Pye and ſhake it, ſo ſend it up hot.

A Partridge Pye.

TAKE your Partridges and ſeaſon them with Pepper, Salt, Cloves, and Mace; then take ſix Cabbage Lettice; boil them four Minutes, ſqueeze the Water well from them; put Puff Paſte in the Diſh, and lay in the Partridges, with a Lettice between every one, and Sauſages: Firſt fry them a little, and put in a Glaſs of white Wine, and a Piece of Butter; cover it with a thick Paſte; bake it two Hours. For the Sauce, have Gravy well ſeaſoned; put it in the Top of the Pye, with a Funnel, and ſhake the Pye; You may put in Claret in ſtead of white Wine, if you pleaſe.

To make a Pye of Mutton and Potatoes.

TAKE a Breaſt of Mutton, and cut it in Steaks; ſeaſon it with Pepper and Salt; lay a Lair of Mutton and a Lair of Potatoes, ſcraped and ſliced, then a Lair of ſliced Onions, ſo go on till you fill the Diſh; ſeaſon them between every Lair; cover it with Puff Paſte two Hours; bake it; put a Piece of ſweet Butter in it, and Gravy, when it comes out of the Oven.

To make a Pye of Kernels and Artichokes.

BLANCH the Kernels, and boil the Artichoke Bottoms; boil Eggs hard, take out the Yolks; put Butter in the Bottom of the Diſh, then the Kernels; then a Lair of Artichoke Bottoms, and a Lair of the Yolks of Eggs: So fill the Diſh in Lairs; ſeaſon them with Pepper, Salt, Cloves, Mace, and Lemon-peel; put Butter over them; then cover it with Puff Paſte; have ready a Ragoo of Truffles, Morels, Gravy, with a little brown'd Butter and Flour, a Glaſs of white Wine, an Onion ſtuffed with Cloves, and the Rind of a Lemon; boil them, then cut off the Top of the Pye, and pour your Ragoo on it; put on the Top again, and ſend it up hot.

To make an Apple Pye with Potatoes.

PEEL and ſlice the Apples, half boil the Potatoes, pare and ſlice them in Lairs in the Diſh with Sugar, Cinnamon, grated Lemon-peel, and a Piece of Butter. You may put Currants, Raiſins, and candied Orange; cover the Pye and bake it. Send it up hot.

To make an Apple Pye with Cheſnuts and Almonds.

Pare and quarter the Apples, ſcald the Cheſnuts, and take off the Skin, blanch the Almonds; lay them in Lairs in the Diſh: Put in candied Orange and Lemon-peel, and fine Sugar; put in a Bit of Butter: When the Apples are full ripe, put in the Juice of a Lemon. Cover it with Puff Paſte: It is to be eaten either hot or cold. If cold, cream it.

To make a white Fricaſey of Lamb.

CUT a Neck and Breaſt of Lamb in middling ſmall Pieces, put them in hot Water to blanch, then put them in cold Water; when they are blanch'd put them in a cloſs cover'd Stew-pan, with a Mutchkin of Water, a Bunch of ſweet Herbs, a whole Onion ſtuffed with Cloves, the Rind of a Lemon, and a Blade of Mace: Lt them ſtew on a gentle Fire till the Meat is enough; then put in a good Piece of Butter work'd in Flour, and a Gill of thick Cream, keep it ſtirring all the while it is on the Fire. After you put in the Butter, when the Rawneſs is off the Flour, put in a Glaſs of Sherry, and the Squeeze of a Lemon. Don't make it too ſour, or put it on the Fire after; ſalt it to your Taſte: Take out the Onion and Herbs, ſo ſerve it up. Garniſh it with Lemons and Muſhrooms.

To make a white Fricaſey of Muſhrooms.

WASH the little white Muſhrooms in Milk and Water, put them down to boil in a little Water and a Blade of Mace, a little white Pepper, with a whole Shalot. When they are tender, put to them a little Cream,

Cream, and a Bit of Butter worked in Flour. When you put them down to boil, put but a very little Water in it, and let them be very closs covered: Just as you are sending them up, put a little white Wine and a very little Lemon Juice, keeping it stirring all the Time.

To fricasey Tripes or Cow-heels.

LET them lye in Souse till they are a little sour, then take them out and dry them with a Cloth; make a Batter of Eggs and Flour and dip them in it, put them in your Pan to fry when the Liquor is boiling hot. The Sauce for them is Butter and Mustard.

To make a white Fricasey of Chickens.

CUT your Chickens in Quarters, then cut every Quarter in two, put them in a Pan with Water to cover them, and give them a Boil or two; then put them in cold Water, take off the Skin and blanch them; put them in a closs covered Pan with Mushrooms, and Truffles with them, a Piece of Butter, a little Flour, a little Salt, a Blade of Mace, a whole Onion stuffed with Cloves, a whole Anchovy, and the Rind of a Lemon; shake the Pan till the Flour mixes, put them on a slow Fire. When they are boil'd enough put in a Gill of thick sweet Cream, and just as you are going to send it up put in a little white Wine, and a very little Juice of Lemons. You may beat the Yolks of two Eggs, and mix them with the Sauce to thicken it, but take great Care not to curdle them. You may make it without Mushrooms, or Truffles, if you please.

To make a Fricasey of Rabbets.

CUT them in Quarters and blanch them as above, then boil them; when they are enough throw off the Water, and put to them some white Gravy, Anchovy, an Onion stuffed with Cloves, Pepper, Salt, Mace, and the Rind of a Lemon, a good Piece of Butter work'd in Flour, and a Bunch of sweet Herbs. Let them boil

a

a good while, then put in a little good Cream, and just as you are going to dish it, put in a little Sherry, and a very little Lemon Juice.

To make a brown Fricasey of Chickens or Rabbets.

BROWN your Butter and Flour, then put in Gravy, shake it that it does not go to Lumps; put in your Meat with Pepper, Cloves, and *Jamaica* Pepper, an Onion and Lemon-peel, put a little Ketchup and the Juice of a Lemon; salt it to your Taste. Garnish them with Lemon.

To fricasey Kernels and Oisters.

BLANCH the Kernels, cut them in Dice, and scald the Oisters, pick and wash them clean in their own Liquor, then put them both in a Stew-pan, with a little white Gravy, and some of the Oister Liquor, strained very clear; an Onion stuffed with Cloves, Mace and Lemon-peel, with a Piece of Butter rolled in Flour, and a Gill of Cream: Give them eight or ten Boils, then shake in a little white Wine and Lemon Juice, but don't put it on the Fire. After the Wine and Juice goes in, take out the Lemon-peel and Onion, then serve it up.

A white Fricasey of Cows Palates.

BOIL, blanch and skin them, then cut them in Shaves the cross Way, as broad as your Finger, put them in a Stew-pan with Mushrooms, Truffles, white Gravy, three whole Shalots, white Pepper, two Anchovies, Salt and Mace, a Piece of Butter, a little Flour, and a Gill of Cream; put them on a slow Fire, and when they are very tender, take them off, and put in a Glass of white Wine, and Lemon Juice: Don't put them on the Fire after. Put Sippets in the Dish under them.

A

A white Fricasey of Lambs Stones, Kernels, and Cocks Combs.

BLANCH and boil the Cocks Combs till they are tender, blanch the Kernels, nick the Skin of the Lambs Stones, and turn them out of the Skins; then blanch them, and put them all in a Pan with Veal Gravy, whole white Pepper, Mace, Salt, and a whole Onion; ſtew them on a ſlow Fire, then put in a little thick Cream, the Grate of a Lemon, and a Bit of ſweet Butter; take it up, and mix it with the Yolks of two Eggs well beaten; then put it on the Fire till it is ſcalding hot; then put in a little white Wine, and ſend it away.

A white Fricaſey of Oiſters.

SCALD them, and waſh them in their own Liquor, then put them in a Pan with ſome white Gravy, and ſome of their own Liquor, Cream, white Pepper, Mace and Salt, a good Piece of Butter rolled in Flour, a whole Onion, and the Rind of a Lemon: Give them a Boil or two, then diſh them on Sippets: You may make a white Fricaſey of Cockles or Scollops the ſame Way.

To fry Chickens, Lamb, or Veal.

CUT the Chickens in Quarters, and your Lamb or Veal in ſmall Joints, put them to ſtew in as much Water as will cover them; ſet them on a ſlow Fire, in a cloſs covered Pan: When they are almoſt enough, put in a good Handful of Parſley, and a few green Onions; then, a little before you take them up, put in four or five Eggs, with pounded Pepper, Salt and Mace, then diſh them up.

A white Fricaſey of Skirrets or Parſnips.

BOIL, blanch and ſkin them, then put them in a Pan, with as much Milk as will cover them, with a good Piece of Butter, white Pepper, Mace pounded, and two whole Onions: Boil them on a ſlow Fire, then

then thicken them with the Yolks of two or three Eggs. The Parsnips and Skirrets must be cut an Inch long. Don't let them boil after you put in the Eggs: You may do Potatoes the same Way: Take out the Onions, and serve them up.

To stew Chickens with Pease and Lettices.

TAKE two Chopins of young Pease, and three Cabbage Lettices; slice the Lettice, and put the Pease in a Sauce-pan, with a Mutchkin of good white Gravy, two Chickens trussed for boiling; rub the Chickens with a Bit of Butter, and put a Piece of Butter in with the Pease; put in a Faggot of sweet Herbs, if you like it; season it with Pepper and Salt; put your Chickens in the Middle of your Dish, and pour the Pease over them: You may stove Lamb or Ducks the same Way.

Boiled Ducks and Onions.

BOIL your Ducks very white, then boil twelve Onions very tender, shifting the Water to take off the Taste; chop them, and draw eight Ounces of Butter, with two Gills of Cream; when it boils, stir in the Onions, and a little Salt, lay your Ducks in the Dish, and pour your Onions over them. Rabbets are done the same Way.

To boil a Turkey or Fowls with Sellery.

BOIL your Turkey or Fowls in a Pot of boiling Water, rub Butter and Flour on the Breasts, and tye them up in a Cloth. You may stuff where their Crops were, thus: Two Handfuls of Crumbs of Bread, one of Sewet shred small, Lemon-peel, Parsley, Thyme, sweet Marjoram, and a little Onion, all shred small; season it with Pepper, Salt and Nutmeg; wet it with an Egg, and work it together, so stuff them full: Cut the Sellery about half an Inch long, wash it clean, and boil it tender; strain it, and put it in as much white Gravy as you want Sauce, with a good Piece of Butter work'd in Flour; season it with an Onion, stuffed with Cloves, Pepper, Salt, Mace, Lemon-peel and Nutmeg; boil it well, then take out the Onion and Lemon-peel, and put in a little white Wine and the Juice of half a Lemon: Don't make it too sour; you may boil Fowls or Turkies, with Oister Sauce to the Meat.

Or this Sauce for Hens or Chickens.

BOIL the Liver, and two Eggs hard, chop them small, mince Parsley and Lemon-peel; then put them all into beat Butter, with Gravy in it, and a little Lemon Juice.

To roast a Pig.

WIPE it very dry, and put in the Belly a Crust of Bread, sew it up, and spit it, drudge it very well with Flour, let it have a very good quick Fire, and let it be very fast turned: When you think it is done, wipe off the Flour, and rub it with a Bit of Butter; it will take an Hour and a Quarter to roast: If large, cut off the Head, and put the Jaws and Ears round the Dish; take out the Brains, and chop them small; put them in a little melted Butter and Gravy, Pepper, Salt, a little Sage chopped very small, and an Egg boiled and chopped small; pour it about the Pig; you may cut it down the Back, or send it whole, but take out the Bread before you send it to Table.

To make a white Fricasey Sauce for boiled Fowls, Chickens or Turkeys.

GET white Broth, boil in it the Rind of a Lemon, an Onion stuffed with Cloves, Mace, whole Pepper and Salt: When it is boiled a while, put in a Gill of Cream and the Yolks of two Eggs beat well together: Keep it stirring one Way on the Fire: Put a Piece of Butter in it, and just as it is going to Table, put the Juice of a Lemon and a little white Wine in

it;

it: Don't make it ſour: Take out the Onion and Lemon-peel.

To make a Mutton Haricot.

TAKE a Neck or Loin of Mutton, cut them in Steaks, fry them a light brown, but not too much: Put to them ſome good Broth, a Faggot of ſweet Herbs, ſome diced Carots and Turnips fried, and three ſmall Cabbage Lettices; ſtew all well together, with ſix ſmall Onions, if you like them; ſeaſon it with Pepper, Salt and Cloves; ſkim off all the Fat, and diſh it up; there is not to be too much Broth in the Diſh.

To roaſt Chickens in Paſte.

TRUSS them as for boiling, ſtuff them with Forc'd-meat, and make as much Puff Paſte as will cover them, then wrap it about the Chickens, with buttered Papers over it, tied at each End: It will take an Hour to roaſt them: You may put a Ragoo of Truffles and Morels, or Gravy and Muſhrooms under them, but take off the Papers. You may do Ducks the ſame Way.

Chickens and Sellery.

BOIL them white, and make the Sauce thus: Boil the white Ends of Sellery, cut it in Pieces an Inch long, ſtrain it, and put it into beat Butter, with Muſhroom and Oiſter Liquor: Then pour it boiling hot over your Chickens.

Chickens farced with Oiſters.

LARD them, then mince Parſley, Truffles, Onions, Muſhrooms and Oiſters; ſeaſon it with Pepper, Salt and Mace; put to it the Yolk of an Egg, and a Piece of Butter; put all this in the Chickens Bellies, then tye both Ends of them, and roaſt them; put a Ragoo of Oiſters about them: You may do Howtoudies, or any white Fowl, the ſame Way.

Chickens

Chickens with Gravy forc'd.

TAKE Sweet-breads, Mushrooms, Anchovies, Marrow or Butter, Lemon-peel and Chives, all cut small; mix them with Crumbs of Bread, Pepper, Salt and Nutmeg; wet them with an Egg, then raise up the Skin of the Breasts of your Fowls, stuff it, and stitch it up again, and lard them: You may fill their Bellies with Oisters, and roast them: Put Gravy under them in the Dish: You may do Pheasants, Turkies, or what Fowl you please, the same Way.

Chickens Royal.

LARD them, and put good Forc'd-meat in their Bellies, and half roast them; then stove them in good Gravy; make a Ragoo of Mushrooms, Morels, Truffles and Cocks Combs; lay the Chickens in the Dish, and pour the Ragoo over them. You may do Pigeons the same Way.

Chickens with Tongues, Colly-flowers and Greens.

BOIL your Chickens in Water and Salt, and your Sheep or Hogs Tongues in another Pot: Skim them, then put the Colly-flowers in the Middle, and a Tongue between every Chicken, and the Greens round them; put melted Butter over them.

To boil Chickens and Asparagus.

BOIL the Chickens white, with Forc'd-meat in their Bellies, cut the Asparagus an Inch long, boil them in Water, then dissolve a little Butter and Salt in Water, with minc'd Parsley; then put in the Asparagus, and boil it better; th cken the Sauce with more Butter, Cream, and a little Flour; season it with white Wine, Nutmeg and Lemon Juice. You may do Sauce for a Fowl the same Way.

To

To roaſt young Turkies.

PUT in their Bellies Forc'd-meat, made of their Livers, ſcalded Oiſters, green Onions, Parſley, mince them all, Crumbs of Bread, Salt, Nutmeg, and grated Lemon-peel; mix them all with a Piece of Butter, and a raw Egg: You may either lard them, or roll them in Shaves of Bacon, then paper and roaſt them; put Gravy in the Diſh with them, and Bread-ſauce in a Sauce-boat made thus: Boil ſome Bread and Water, with a little white Gravy, an Onion ſtuffed with Cloves, a Blade of Mace, and a little Salt; boil it ſmooth; put in it a good Lump of Butter, then give it a Boil; take out the Onion before you ſend it to Table. You may roaſt Chickens the ſame Way.

Ducklings à la Mode.

CUT them in Quarters; you may lard the Legs, and brown them off; then ſtove them in half a Mutchkin of Claret, the ſame of Gravy, two Shalots, one Anchovy, Pepper and Salt; ſtove them tender, ſkim off the Fat, ſqueeze in a Lemon, ſo ſerve it up hot.

Stov'd Ducks the Dutch *Way.*

TRUSS two Ducks, and lard one; ſeaſon with Pepper and Salt, and fill the Bellies with ſmall Onions; lay in the Bottom of the Stew-pan half a Pound of Butter; then put in the Ducks, and cover them with ſliced Onions: Stove this two Hours gently, keeping it covered all the while; when the Ducks are tender, diſh them, ſhaking a little Vinegar in them.

To dreſs a Wild-duck with Lemon Juice.

HALF roaſt the Duck, and carve it; on the Breaſt put Salt, Pepper, and the Juice of a Lemon in every Inciſion; lay it on the Breaſt in a Stew-pan, with a very little Gravy; then turn it and diſh it hot in its own Gravy, a Glaſs of Claret, and two Shalots ſhred ſmall.

To stew Ducks, wild or tame.

HALF roast them, then put them in a Stew-pan with two Gills of Claret, and four of Gravy, Pepper, Salt, Shalots, or Rockambole; cover them close: You may stuff the Ducks with Forc'd-meat, and make a Ragoo of Sheeps Tongues, Truffles, and Morels. Serve them up hot with the Breast up, and the Sauce that they were stewed in about them, with all the Ingredients.

To dress Ducks with Oisters.

TAKE Ducks, wild or tame, truss them; make a Ragoo of Sweet-breads, Oisters, Mushrooms, Truffles, Chives, Parsley, Crumbs of Bread, Lemon-peel, Pepper, Salt, and Eggs; stuff the Ducks with it, and stew them in a closs covered Pan, with Gravy, Claret, browned Butter and Flour, Pepper, Salt, Shalot, or Onions; put Oisters fried in Butter about them in the Dish, with the Liquor they are stewed in. You do Teal or Widgeon the same Way.

To roast a green Goose.

STUFF it with Bread Forc'd-meat; roast it crisp, and let the Sauce be a little Spinage Juice, scalded Goosberries, a Bit of Butter, Flour, Sugar, or Gravy, and green Onions shred small. You may give young Ducks the same Sauce.

To dress a Goose with Onions or Cabbage.

SALT it for a Week, then boil it an Hour; make the Sauce of boil'd Onions, chopped small, mixed with melted Butter; or, you may boil Cabbage, and chop and stew them in Butter, Pepper, and Salt; dish the Goose, and put the Onions or Cabbage about it, with fried Sausages.

To souse a Goose.

BONE your Goose, cut the Flesh square; lay it a steeping in white Wine, Salt, Pepper, Cloves, and Mace,

Mace, for twelve Hours; then take it out, and lay Pieces of Anchovies over it; and Ham minced ſmall; then roll it up hard, and boil it in boiling Water, and the Wine it was ſteeped in, with Salt, Pepper, and Mace; boil it pretty well, then put it in a Can, and when you are going to ſerve it up, cut it in two, and lay over it green Parſley.

To dry a Gooſe.

GET a fat Gooſe, and ſalt it well with a Handful of common Salt, a quarter of an Ounce of Salt-petre, a quarter of a Pound of coarſe Sugar; mix all together, and rub the Gooſe very well; let it lye in this Pickle a Fortnight, turning and rubbing it every Day; then roll it in Brawn, then hang it to dry for a Week; it will keep three Months in a dry Place: It eats well cold, or hot, but boil it well in a large Pot full of Water: If eaten hot, ſend Cabbage, or Greens, about it.

To boil a Gooſe.

PUT it in a Pot with Water, or Broth; let it boil, and ſkim it clean; put in a little Salt, three ſliced Onions, a few Cloves, Mace, Raiſins, Currants, and Crumbs of Bread; ſtew it on a ſlow Fire, diſh it on Sippets; put a little white Wine in it, and put Slices of Lemon, and Barberries over it.

To boil the Gibblets.

BLANCH them, then boil them in Water, Salt, and Mace; ſerve them up on Sippets, with melted Butter, and ſcalded Grapes.

To roaſt a Gooſe.

STUFF it with boiled Potatoes, and Onions, chopped ſmall, ſeaſoned with Pepper and Salt; or, you may ſtuff it with Apples, or roaſt it without any Stuffing; but ſeaſon it high, and roaſt it an Hour and a Quarter a Quarter. Put Gravy in the Dish, and Apple Sauce in a Bowl.

To roast Partridges.

AS they are roasting, baste them well and drudge them; put Gravy in the Dish under them, and make a Sauce thus: Boil some thin Slices of fine stale Bread in as much Water as will make it thick and smooth, with whole Pepper, Mace, and an Onion stuffed with Cloves: When it is smooth, put in a good Piece of Butter; stir it and give it a Boil or two, put in a little Salt, so send it in a Sauce-boat with your Partridges. You may lard them, if you please.

To dress Partridges à la Braise.

TRUSS their Legs into their Bodies; give them a Scald, then lard them; season with Pepper, Salt, Cloves, and Mace, sweet Herbs, Chives, and Parsley, all shred; take a Stew-pan with a Cover, lay Slices of Bacon in it, then thin Slices of Beef over them, with Slices of Carots and Onions, Parsley, sweet Herbs, Pepper, Cloves, and Mace; then lay in the Partridges on their Breasts, and lay over them Slices of Beef, then Slices of Bacon; cover the Stew-pan, and let them stew with Fire over and under them; make a Ragoo of Cocks Combs, Livers of fat Fowls, Sweet-breads, Truffles, Mushrooms, Artichoke Bottoms, and Asparagus Tops, according to the Season; when your Partridges are stewed enough, take them up, drain them and dish them with the Ragoo about them; or, you may send them up with a Ragoo of Cucumbers, made thus: Pare and slice them, and some Shalots; put them between two Plates, with a little Pepper and Salt, for two Minutes; then drain off the Liquor that comes from them; then put them in a close covered Pan with a Piece of Butter, and let them stew on a slow Fire till they are soft; then shake in a little Flour and Gravy, keeping them stiring

all

all the while. Put in a chopped Anchovy, and a Spoonful of Ketchup.

Partridges with Oisters.

THEY must be very fresh, draw them; mince their Livers, and some scalded Oisters, the Yolks of hard Eggs, Parsley, sweet Herbs, and Shalots, shred small; Pepper, Salt, and Cloves; work them in a Piece of Butter, and stuff your Partridges with it; roll them up in Slices of Bacon, and Paper, spit them; then get some more Oisters, blanch and pick them; put them in some of their own Liquor, a little good Gravy, a Bit of Butter roll'd in Flour, a Glass of white Wine, the Juice of half a Lemon with the Peel; Shalots cut small, pounded Mace, Pepper, and Salt; boil it, and dish your Partridges, and pour it round them.

To hash Partridges.

HALF roast your Partridges, cut them in Quarters, and joint the Breast and Rump asunder; put them in a Stew-pan, with some good Gravy, the Rind of a Lemon, an Onion stuffed with Cloves, Pepper, Salt, Mace, Truffles, and Morels; a Piece of Butter roll'd in Flour, a Glass of white Wine, and some Lemon Juice; let them all stew on the Fire a Quarter of an Hour, then dish them.

To roast Pheasants.

BLANCH and lard them with Bacon, then roll them in buttered Papers; roast them at a slow Fire: When almost done, take off the Papers to let them have a Colour, and dish them with good Gravy; send the same Bread-sauce as for Partridges, in a Sauce-boat with them. You may send either Oisters or Sellery Sauce with them.

To boil Pheasants, Partridges, Chickens, or Quails.

PUT them in a Stew-pan with as much Water as will cover them, with Mace, Nutmeg, Cloves, a Piece of of Butter, and ſome Crumbs of Bread; Lemon-peel, Onions, and white Wine; let them all ſtew on a ſlow Fire till enough; then take out the Lemon-peel and Onion; turn your Fowl very often; put in the Yolks of hard Eggs, chopped very fine with a little more Butter; give it a Boil, then diſh them all up. Put in the Juice of a Lemon.

A Pupton of Pigeons.

TAKE ſavoury Forc'd-meat rolled out like Paſte, in a butter'd Diſh; lay Pigeons over it, then Sweet-breads and Muſhrooms, then another Roll of Forc'd-meat; cover it and bake it: When enough, turn it on another Diſh, and your Gravy over it. Send it up hot.

Pigeons boiled with Rice.

STUFF their Bellies with chopped Parſley, Pepper and Salt rolled in a Bit of Butter; put them into a Chopin of Broth, with a little beat Mace, a Bunch of ſweet Herbs, and an Onion; cover them cloſe, and let them ſtew for a Quarter of an Hour; then take out the Onion and ſweet Herbs, and take a good Piece of Butter rolled in Flour, put it in and keep it ſtirring till the Butter is diſſolved; then have ready half a Pound of Rice boiled tender, put it to the Pigeons, with Salt and Nutmeg, give them a Scald; then put the Pigeons in the Diſh, and pour the Rice over them.

To ſtew Pigeons.

STUFF them with Forc'd-meat, then half roaſt them; then put them in a Stew-pan, with a Chopin of Gravy, a little white Wine, or Claret, Pepper, Cloves, Salt, Mace, Lemon-peel, pickled Muſhrooms, and Oiſters ſcalded and picked, with ſome of their Liquor and a ſcored Onion; let them ſtew till they are done; thicken the Sauce with Butter and Flour; take out the Onion, and ſend it up hot. You may do Ducks the ſame Way.

To

To fry Pigeons.

BLANCH them and cut them in two, beat them flat, and put them in a Stew-pan, with Onions, Parsley, Pepper, Salt, Cloves, a Piece of Butter, a Ladleful of Broth, or the Liquor they were in; let all these stew a little while, take them out and dip them in Batter made of Eggs and Flour, then fry them; dish them, and pour over them the Liquor they were stewed in, but strain it first: Put the Juice of a Lemon in it.

To broil Pigeons.

YOU may either broil them whole, or slit them down the Back; salt and pepper them; lay them on the Brander, broil them gently, and turn them often; make the Sauce of Butter, their Livers boiled and chopped with Parsley and Shalot: You may put a little red Wine in it and Lemon Juice. If you do them whole, put Forc'd-meat in them.

To boil Pigeons.

PUT them in warm Water to blanch, then boil them in Salt and Water fifteen Minutes; boil a Piece of Bacon, and take off the Skin; then put Crumbs of Bread on it, and lay it before the Fire; boil Spinage, Greens, or Colly-flowers; put the Bacon in the Dish, then the Pigeons, and the Garden things about it. You may dress any tame Fowl the same Way: Don't put Salts in the Collyflowers when you boil them.

To do Pigeons à la Daube.

STUFF their Bellies with Forc'd-meat made thus: Take a Pound of Veal, and a Pound of Beef Sewet; beat it in a Mortar, and season it with Pepper, Salt, and Nutmeg; put as much Crumbs of Bread as Sewet; brown them in clarified Butter, then shake in a little Flour, and put in it some good Gravy, and Onion stuffed with Cloves, Pepper, Salt, Mace, and Lemon-

peel;

peel; let them stew a while: Put a Ragoo of any Sort about them, or the Liquor they are stewed in.

Pigeons stoved with Cabbage Lettice.

STUF them as before; season them with Pepper, Salt, and Cloves; brown them with Butter, then put them to stove with Cabbage Lettice cut in Quarters, and two green Onions, a little Gravy, a Glass of Wine, and some Lemon Juice; let them all stew on a slow Fire, then dish them. Put Forc'd-meat Balls and Lemon about them.

Pigeons disguised.

SEASON them with Pepper and Salt; make Puff Paste, and roll each Pidgeon in Paste; tye them in a Cloth; boil them in a good Deal of Water for an Hour; untye them carefully that they don't break; dish them and pour Gravy about them. So serve them up hot.

A stewed Pheasant.

STEW it in white Gravy, and when it is almost enough, put in it Salt, Pepper and Mace, then take boiled Artichoke Bottoms, Chesnuts roasted and skinned, and put them in with a good Piece of Butter rolled in Flour, a Glass of white Wine and Lemon Juice: Let them stew a while, then dish your Pheasant and Sauce; put Forc'd-meat Balls or Sausages about it: A good Fowl will do as well, but truss it with the Head on like a Pheasant.

To roast Growse, or what is called Moor-fowl.

TWO makes a Dish; lard one of them, then spit and roast them well; for the Sauce, take good brown Gravy, Crumbs of Bread browned in a Pan, with a very little Bit of Butter, a Gill of Claret, a shred Shalot, Pepper and Salt.

To

To fry Pigeons.

BLANCH them and cut them in two, beat them flat, and put them in a Stew-pan, with Onions, Parsley, Pepper, Salt, Cloves, a Piece of Butter, a Ladleful of Broth, or the Liquor they were in; let all these stew a little while, take them out and dip them in Batter made of Eggs and Flour, then fry them; dish them, and pour over them the Liquor they were stewed in, but strain it first: Put the Juice of a Lemon in it.

To broil Pigeons.

YOU may either broil them whole, or slit them down the Back; salt and pepper them; lay them on the Brander, broil them gently, and turn them often; make the Sauce of Butter, their Livers boiled and chopped with Parsley and Shalot: You may put a little red Wine in it and Lemon Juice. If you do them whole, put Forc'd-meat in them.

To boil Pigeons.

PUT them in warm Water to blanch, then boil them in Salt and Water fifteen Minutes; boil a Piece of Bacon, and take off the Skin; then put Crumbs of Bread on it, and lay it before the Fire; boil Spinage, Greens, or Colly-flowers; put the Bacon in the Dish, then the Pigeons, and the Garden things about it. You may dress any tame Fowl the same Way: Don't put Salts in the Collyflowers when you boil them.

To do Pigeons à la Daube.

STUFF their Bellies with Forc'd-meat made thus: Take a Pound of Veal, and a Pound of Beef Sewet; beat it in a Mortar, and season it with Pepper, Salt, and Nutmeg; put as much Crumbs of Bread as Sewet; brown them in clarified Butter, then shake in a little Flour, and put in it some good Gravy, and Onion stuffed with Cloves, Pepper, Salt, Mace, and Lemon-

peel;

peel; let them ſtew a while: Put a Ragoo of any Sort about them, or the Liquor they are ſtewed in.

Pigeons ſtoved with Cabbage Lettice.

STUF them as before; ſeaſon them with Pepper, Salt, and Cloves; brown them with Butter, then put them to ſtove with Cabbage Lettice cut in Quarters, and two green Onions, a little Gravy, a Glaſs of Wine, and ſome Lemon Juice: let them all ſtew on a ſlow Fire, then diſh them. Put Forc'd-meat Balls and Lemon about them.

Pigeons diſguiſed.

SEASON them with Pepper and Salt; make Puff Paſte, and roll each Pidgeon in Paſte; tye them in a Cloth; boil them in a good Deal of Water for an Hour; untye them carefully that they don't break; diſh them and pour Gravy about them. So ſerve them up hot.

A ſtewed Pheaſant.

STEW it in white Gravy, and when it is almoſt enough, put in it Salt, Pepper and Mace, then take boiled Artichoke Bottoms, Cheſnuts roaſted and ſkinned, and put them in with a good Piece of Butter rolled in Flour, a Glaſs of white Wine and Lemon Juice: Let them ſtew a while, then diſh your Pheaſant and Sauce; put Forc'd-meat Balls or Sauſages about it: A good Fowl will do as well, but truſs it with the Head on like a Pheaſant.

To roaſt Growſe, or what is called Moor-fowl.

TWO makes a Diſh; lard one of them, then ſpit and roaſt them well; for the Sauce, take good brown Gravy, Crumbs of Bread browned in a Pan, with a very little Bit of Butter, a Gill of Claret, a ſhred Shalot, Pepper and Salt.

To

To roaſt Snipes or Woodcocks.

DON'T draw them, ſlit them a-croſs, toaſt ſome Bread, and lay it in a Plate under them, that the Trale may drop in it: When roaſted well, lay them on the toaſted Bread, and pour beat Butter with Gravy over them: Send them up hot.

To ſtew Larks, or any other ſmall Birds.

TOSS them in a Stew-pan with ſome Butter, an Onion ſtuck with Cloves, ſome Muſhrooms, and the Livers of the Birds, with a little Gravy: Let them ſtew on a ſlow Fire; then beat two Eggs, with ſome ſhred Parſley; mix it by Degrees with the Sauce; put in ſome Salt and the Grate of a Lemon. Juſt as it is going to be diſhed, put in a little Lemon Juice.

To roaſt Larks.

PUT them on a Skewer, tye them to the Spit, baſte them and drudge them with Crumbs of Bread and Salt; then have Crumbs of Bread, and lay it in the Diſh with them.

To roaſt Curlews.

WHEN they are gutted, thruſt them like a Woodcock, ſeaſon them with Pepper and Salt: You may put Forc'd-meat in them, roaſt them well, baſte and drudge them, put Gravy, Claret and Orange Juice in the Diſh under them.

To roaſt Quails.

STUFF their Bellies with Crumbs of Bread, chopped Parſley, Shalot, Oiſters, and ſweet Marjoram; put a Piece of Butter in it, and a raw Egg, all work'd up together; then ſpit and roaſt them: When done, put Gravy, Anchovy, and the Juice of a Lemon in the Diſh under them.

To

To roast Plovers.

PUT into their Bellies, Pepper, Salt, chopped Anchovies and Shalots: Don't roast them too much, and put good Gravy under them in the Dish.

To stew Plovers.

SEASON them with Pepper, Salt and Cloves, put them in a Stew-pan with Gravy and Shalots; put them on a slow Fire; when they are half done, skim off all the Fat, and strain it, then put into it two Gills of Claret, and an Onion stuffed with Cloves; then stove them till they are done; dish them, and pour the Sauce over them. You may do wild Ducks, Teals or Widgeons the same Way. Take out the Onion.

A jugged Hare.

CUT it in Pieces, lard the Quarters with Bacon, put it in a Can that has a very narrow Mouth, with whole Pepper, Cloves and Mace: Cover the Can close, that the Steam cannot come out; then put it in a Pot of Water, and let it boil in it three Hours, still filling the Pot with Water up to the Can's Neck, but not as high as it can get into it. You may put Onions and a Faggot of sweet Herbs in it, if you please; then put it in the Dish, salt it to your Taste, and take out the Herbs and Onions.

To roast a Hare.

LARD the Hare, and put a Stuffing in the Belly, with Crumbs of Bread, the Heart, Beef Sewet and the Liver chopped small, Parsley, Onion and sweet Herbs shred fine; season it with Pepper, Salt, Nutmeg, and the Grate of a Lemon; wet it with an Egg, then sew it up and spit it, and baste it with Cream till all the Blood is sok'd out: Let it dry, then flour and salt it, and baste it with Butter: For Sauce, you may give it beat Butter, Gravy and Claret Sauce in a Boat.

To roast a Hare another Way.

LARD the Hare, take grated Bread, Eggs, Currants, Nutmeg, Cinnamon, Sugar, and a little Cream: Make all these in a Pudding, stirring it in a Pan on the Fire for six Minutes; then put it in the Hare's Belly, sew it up, spit it, roast it, and baste it with Butter. You may give it Claret Sauce and beat Butter.

To roast a Hare with the Skin on.

TAKE out the Bowels, wipe the Inside with a Cloth, put a Pudding in it, of either savoury or sweet, as before; sew the Belly up, then loosen all the Skin, and rub Butter all over the Flesh; then sew up the Skin, and roast it, basting it with boiling Water and Salt, till it is half roasted, then let it dry; and when it smokes, pull it off by Pieces, then baste it with Butter, and drudge it with Flour or grated Bread. The Sauce is beat Butter, or Gravy and Claret.

To hash a Hare.

HALF roast it, then cut it in Quarters, put it in a Stew-pan, with Pepper, Salt, Cloves, Lemon-peel, whole Onions, a Bunch of sweet Herbs, and a little Gravy and Claret. You may thicken it a little with brown'd Butter and Flour: Take out the Lemon-peel, sweet Herbs and Onions.

To mince a Hare.

WHEN there is any Hare left that has been roasted, mince it small, put it in a Stew-pan, with two Gills of good Gravy, a little Parsley, Lemon-peel, Onions and scalded Oisters, all shred small, a Piece of Butter rolled in Flour, Pepper, Salt and Mace, a Glass of white Wine, and a little Lemon Juice: Give it two or three Boils, keeping it stirring all the Time, then send it up hot; or you may half roast it, and then hash it the same Way.

To

To boil Rabbets.

LET them ſteep in warm Water a Quarter of an Hour, then put them in a Pot of boiling Water and Salt. Three Quarters of an Hour boils them. For the Sauce, you may boil Onions, chop them, and mix them with a Gill of Cream and a good Piece of Butter; pour it over them boiling hot, and put Salt in it; or you may boil the Livers, chop them with Parſley and Pickles, mix them with a Gill of Gravy, a good Piece of Butter rolled in Flour, and a little white Wine ſeaſoned with Pepper, Salt, Mace and Nutmeg. You may lard them with Bacon if you like it.

Boiled Rabbets with Sauſages.

STEW the Rabbets in as much Water as will cover them, with Pepper, Salt, Cloves, Onions and ſweet Herbs. When half done, take out the Rabbets, and ſtrain the Broth, then blanch ſome Lettice and Spinage, and put them and the Rabbets in the Broth, with a Piece of Butter rolled in Flour, ſome Muſhrooms or Truffles, if you have them: Fry Sauſages, and when you diſh the Rabbets and Sauce, put the Sauſages about them. When you roaſt Rabbets, beat Butter, their own Liver, and Parſley minced ſmall, is the Sauce.

To ſtew Rabbets the French *Way.*

CUT them in Quarters, lard them with Bacon, then ſtew them in ſtrong Gravy, with a little white Wine, Pepper, Salt and Mace, browned Butter and Flour, and the Juice of a Lemon. Send them hot to Table.

To collar Salmon.

TAKE a Side of Salmon, cut a Piece of the Tail, rub the other Piece with Eggs, make a Forc'd-meat of the Tail, chop it ſmall, with a Handful of Oiſters that is parboiled, the Yolks of ſix Eggs boiled hard, and two Anchovies; chop them all ſmall; ſeaſon it with Pepper, Salt, Mace, Nutmeg, and ſome grated Bread; work them

them up with two raw Eggs, and lay it all over the Salmon, but first season it with all the Spices as above. Roll it up in a Collar, and bind it with broad Tape, and boil it in boiling Water, Salt and Vinegar, for two Hours on a slow Fire, then take it out and let it cool, and skim all the Fat off the Water it was boiled in; take off the Bindings of the Collar, and when both is cold, put it in the Water it was boiled in.

To collar Pork.

TAKE a Piece of Pork and bone it, strew it with Salt, Pepper, Cloves, Mace, Parsley, Sage, Thyme and sweet Marjoram, all shred small; then cut Slices off a Leg of Veal, and season them as above. Lay them in the Pork, rub them and the Inside of the Pork with raw Eggs, then roll it up in a Collar very hard, bind it with broad Tapes, and put it in a large Pot of boiling Water. It will take three Hours boiling, then take it out of the Pot, and when it is cold, you may make Use of it, and keep it in the same Souse you do Brawn.

To collar a Pig.

CUT off the Head and Feet, and slit it down the Belly, take out all the Intrails, bone it, and lay it in Water to soke out the Blood, then dry it with a Cloth, season it with chopped Sage and Parsley, white Pepper, Salt and Mace, roll it up very hard, and roll a Cloth about it; tye both Ends, put it in a Pot of boiling Water, with a little Salt in it. It will, if large, take an Hour and a Half to boil it: When you take it out of the Pot, hang it up by one End till it is almost cold: You may send it to Table either whole or in Slices.

To collar a Fore-quarter of Lamb, or a Breast of Veal.

BONE them, and season them with chopped Parsley and sweet Herbs, black and *Jamaica* Pepper, Cloves and Salt; roll them up hard, and bind them with a Cloth tied at both Ends, put them in boiling

Water. The Lamb will take an Hour and three Quarters, but the Veal will take but an Hour and a Half: Hang them by one End, till almost cold, then take them out of the Cloth.

To collar Cow Heels.

WHEN the Hair is well cleaned off the Feet, boil them till the Bones come out, then season them with black and *Jamaica* Pepper, and Salt, roll them up tight, and boil them half an Hour more in their own Broth; hang them up till almost cold, then take them out of the Cloth.

To collar a Calf's Head.

CUT your Head in two, and wash and soke it in warm Water, put it to boil, and when the Bones come out, season it with Salt, Cloves, Pepper and Mace; then shread sweet Marjoram, Thyme and Parsley, and strew them on it; put the thin Part of one Side to the thick Part of the other, roll it up, and boil it for an Hour in its own Broth, then take it out, and hang it up till almost cold, then take it out of the Cloth.

To make a very good Collar of a Hog's Head.

WHEN it is clean washed, put it down to boil, and a Set of Cow Heels down with it; when boiled, take out all the Bones, and season them with black and *Jamaica* Pepper, and Salt; cut out the black of the Eye, put your Feet in the Middle, and roll it up very tight in a Cloth, boil it in its own Broth an Hour, hang it up by one End, and when almost cold, take it out of the Cloth. You may collar a Cow's Head the same Way, leaving out the Feet.

To collar Eels.

GET large Eels, cut off the Head and Fins, bone them, season them with black and *Jamaica* Pepper, Cloves and Salt; roll them up very hard, and put them down

down to boil in Water, Salt and Vinegar, with a few Bay Leaves: Boil them ſo tender, that you may thruſt a Straw in them; take them out, and boil the Liquor better, with whole Spice in it. Let it cool, and ſkim off all the Fat; then put in your Eels in your cold Liquor.

To pot a Cow's Head.

LET it blanch in Water all Night, then put it to boil, and when it is enough, all the Bones will come out; take out the Black out of the Eyes, and cut it in thin Bits; ſeaſon them with Pepper, Salt, Cloves, and Mace; lay all the Bits in any Thing that will bear the Fire: You may have it in what Shape you pleaſe, according to what you bake it in: Mind to put a Bit of Fat and Lean always together in different Pieces, one on the other; clarify a Chopin of the Broth it was boiled in, and when your Bits are all laid in your Can, pour it over them: You may put a Gill of white Wine and a Gill of Vinegar in it; cover the Can cloſe, and bake it two Hours: When it comes out of the Oven, put a light Weight on it, and when cold take it out: You may ſend it to Table either whole or in Slices. It is to be eaten with Muſtard and Vinegar cold.

To pot Pigeons.

CUT off the Feet and Wings; ſeaſon them with Salt and Pepper; chop the Liver and Gizzard very ſmall, mix a good Handful of Crumbs of Bread with them, a little Parſley, Onion, and Lemon-peel ſhred ſmall; a good Piece of Butter; wet it with an Egg; work it up together, and put it in the Pigeons Bellies; then put them in a Can with a good Piece of Butter; cover it cloſe, and put it in the Oven: It is better than doing them on the Fire. You may do them without ſtuffing, if you pleaſe: But you muſt put Butter in their Bellies if you take them out of the Veſſel that they were baked in, and put them in ſmall Pots, they

will

will keep a long while; but you must drain all the Gravy from them, and put clarified Butter over them.

To make Liver Puddings.

HALF boil a Hog's Draught, mince it very small; to every Pound of it put a Pound of the Hog's Lard cut small, or a Pound of Beef Sewet; you must put a Pound of Crumbs of Bread in it; season it with Pepper, Salt, and Clove Pepper: You may put Currants in them, if you please; wet it with a very little Water; fill and boil them as you do the Blood Puddings: If you put Currants in them, put a little Sugar too.

The proper Sauces for wild Fowl.

DUCKS, Veal, and Plover must be roasted very well; the Sauce is Gravy, Crumbs of Bread, Shalots, and a little Claret; season it with Pepper and Salt. Partridges and Moor-fowl must be very well roasted. Their Sauce is a little Bread boil'd in Water, a Blade of Mace, an Onion stuff'd with Cloves, a good Piece of Butter, and a little Salt: You may put a little white Wine and Ketchup in it. Woodcocks and Snipes are roasted well, with their Guts in them; put toasted Bread, and beat Butter under them: Under other Fowls put Gravy; and put about any small Birds fried Crumbs only. The proper Sauce for roasted Venison is Claret boiled very thick, with Sugar or Currant Jelly.

To pot Woodcocks, or Snipes.

DON'T take out the Trale; season them with Salt and Clove Pepper; put them in a Can with a good deal of sweet Butter; cover it close, and bake them; when baked, take them out of the Can, and let all the Butter drain from them; put them in small Pots, clarify the Butter they were in; add more to it, and pour it on them: Don't let any of the Gravy be in it. They must be covered with Butter.

To

To pot a Hare.

ROAST or bake the Hare, and when cold, pull all the Flesh from the Bones; pound it and season it with Pepper, Salt, Cloves, and Mace; put in an equal Quantity of sweet Butter as you have of Hare; clarify the Butter, and mix it with the Hare, then put it in small Pots; and when cold, pour clarified Butter on it: You may send it to Table in these Pots. You may pot Moor-fowl or Partridges the same Way.

To pot a Calf's Head.

BOIL it and two Calves Feet in as much Water as will cover them, with Pepper, Salt, Cloves, and Lemon-peel; boil it till the bones come out, then strew on it a little Salt; boil the Broth it was boiled in till it is in a very stiff Jelly; cut the Head in thin Slices, the Breadth of a Crown; skin the Tongue and Palates, and slice them; cut the Eyes in round Rings; place them all regular in a Bowl that will bear the Oven; then take the Broth, and put in it whole Pepper, Cloves, Mace, and Lemon-peel, and the Juice of a Lemon, or a little Vinegar; clarify it with the Whites of two Eggs, and let it run through a Jelly-bag; then pour it over the Head, and put it in the Oven for half an Hour. The Oven must not be hot.

To pot Beef.

TAKE the Lean off a Buttock of Beef; cut some thin Pieces, and rub it with Salt-petre; let it lye in it three Days, then dry it with a Cloth; put it in a flat Can, with Butter over and under it, cover the Can close with coarse Paste; put it in the Oven for four Hours, then take it out and drain all the Butter and Gravy from the Beef; and when it is cold, and very clean of all the Fat, string it and pound it very fine; rub it thro' a coarse Search, then season it with white Pepper, Cloves, Mace, and Salt; to every Pound of the Beef, after it is put through the Search, put a Pound

of

of clarified Butter, ſkim it clean, and pour it from the Bottom, that none of the Milk or Sediment go in it; then mix it with the Beef, and put it in ſmall white Tart-pans; and when it is cold, pour clarified Butter over it. You may pot Veniſon the ſame Way.

To pot Tongues.

PICKLE them red, as you do to dry, then boil them tender, and peel them; rub them with Pepper, Cloves, and Mace; then turn them round on their Side in Pots that will hold but one; cover them with Butter; bake them when they come out of the Oven, pour off all the Gravy, and put the Butter that was over them and more clarified Butter over them. They will keep a great while.

To pot Veniſon.

TAKE a Piece of Veniſon, Fat and Lean together, lay it in a Diſh, and put Pieces of Butter over it; tye over the Diſh ſome coarſe Paper or brown Dough; put it in the Oven, and bake it very well, then take it out of the Gravy, and when it is cold and well drained, pound it, both Fat and Lean, but firſt ſkin and bone it; ſeaſon it with Salt, Pepper, Cloves, Nutmeg and Mace, all pounded fine; then clarify the Butter that it was baked in, with as much added to it as will moiſten it, and put it in ſmall potting Pots; You muſt be ſure to take out all the Strings, and let it be beat to a Paſte. Cover the Pots with clarified Butter.

To pot Beef or Veniſon in Slices.

TAKE lean Beef, and cut it in Slices, beat them with the Roller, and lard them; ſeaſon them with Pepper, Salt, Cloves and Mace; put them in a Diſh, and bake them with Butter over them; cover them cloſe. You may put Onions and ſweet Herbs to them, if you pleaſe. They are to be eaten either hot or cold.

To pot Salmon the Newcaſtle *Way.*

TAKE the Salmon, and ſcale and wipe it very clean, but don't waſh it; ſalt it well, then let it ly till the Salt is melted and drained from it, then ſeaſon it with Pepper, Cloves and Mace: Put it in a Pot with Butter over it, cover it cloſs, and bake it: When baked, pour all the Gravy from it; and when it is cold, put clarified Butter over it. You may do Carp, Tench, Trouts, and ſeveral Kinds of Fiſh, the ſame Way.

To pot a Pike.

SCALE it, and cut off the Head, ſplit it, take out the Bones, wipe it clean, and ſalt the Inſide with Bay, Salt and Pepper; roll it up round, and put it in a Pot with Butter over it; cover it cloſs, bake it an Hour, then pour all the Liquor from it, and lay it to drain on a a Cloth, then put it in a potting Pot, and pour clarified Butter on it.

To make Marrow Paſties.

CUT half a Pound of Marrow in Bits, ſhread ſix Apples, and the Yolks of three hard Eggs, a Pound of Currants, pick them clean, plump them before the Fire, and mix all together; ſeaſon it with the Grate of a Lemon, pounded Cinnamon, Mace, Nutmeg, a very little Sugar and Salt: Put them in Puff Paſte. You may either bake or fry them.

To dreſs a Veal or Lamb's Ear, properly called Kidneys.

SLIT the Kidneys, Fat and all, rub it with an Egg, ſtrew on it Crumbs of Bread, Parſley, Thyme, Onion, Pepper and Salt; fry it in a Pan. You may mince it if you pleaſe, and ſeaſon it with Sugar, Nutmeg, and a little Salt; waſh a few Currants in warm Water, and plump them before the Fire: Mix all together with the Grate of a Lemon, roll a little Puff Paſte, and fry them in it. You may make them without Sugar or

Currants, if you please; and if you put an Egg in them, you may do them on Toasts before the Fire.

To make Blood Puddings.

WHEN the Beast is killing, stir the Blood with your Hand, and break the Lumps: Put Salt in it; while hot, strain it, boil a Chopin of Groats in Milk, and put them in when they both are cold. To every Pint of this, put a Pound of chopped Sewet, shred sweet Herbs and Onions; season it to your Taste with Pepper and Salt, clean the Skins very well, fill three Parts of them, tye them, have a Pot of boiling Water, and put them in: Let them not boil at first, but take them out and prick them a little to let out the Wind: When they are almost cold, put them in again. Do this three or four Times, till they are a little hard, then they won't burst in the boiling; stir them in the Skins when you are putting them first down.

To make a Yorkshire Pudding.

BEAT eight Eggs, and beat in them a Pound of Flour, putting a Mutchkin of Milk in by Degrees in it; shread half a Pound of Beef Sewet very fine, and mix in it; season it with Salt and Ginger; three Hours boils it. You may bake a Pudding made the same Way.

To make a Plumb Pudding.

BEAT eight Eggs and half a Pound of Flour, two Gills of Milk, and half a Pound of Raisins shred, half a Pound of Currants washed and picked clean, half a Pound of Beef Sewet shred small, and mix all together; season it with Nutmeg, Ginger, Salt, and a Glass of Brandy. Two Hours boils it.

To make Almond Puddings in Lemon or Orange Skins.

BOIL your Skins, first cut a Hole on the Top, and take out all the Inside, boil them tender in Water, then boil them in Syrup; blanch a Quarter of a Pound

Pound of ſweet Almonds, and four bitter ones; pound them fine, mix them with a Gill of Cream, two Eggs, and two Spunge Biſcuits; crumb them ſmall; ſeaſon it with Sugar to your Taſte, put them in a Sauce-pan, and ſtir them one Way on the Fire, till the Rawneſs is off the Eggs: Take care it does not curdle; then fill your Skins, and put the Bit that you cut out in its Place again. This is enough for an Aſhet. Send them hot to the Table.

To make a Peaſe Pudding.

TAKE a Pound of ſplit Peaſe, and tye them in a Cloth, giving them Room to ſwell. Let them boil an Hour, then take them up, and blend them with a Spoon, put in them a good Piece of Butter, a little Salt and Pepper. Put them again in the Pot, let them boil half an Hour, and put beat Butter about them.

To make an Almond Pudding.

BLANCH and pound half a Pound of ſweet Almonds, and ſix bitter ones, very fine, keeping them wetting as they are pounding with Brandy or Ratafia; beat the Yolks of twelve Eggs to a Cream, and pound and ſift half a Pound of Sugar, and mix it with your Eggs by Degrees, keeping them whiſking all the Time; then your Almonds, then put in ſix Ounces of oiled Butter; put it in the Oven as ſoon as you can, with Puff Paſte about the Diſh. You may make half the Quantity of any of theſe Puddings, if you pleaſe to try them, but put them in a very ſmall Aſhet. They are all approved Receipts.

To make a Citron Pudding.

POUND five Ounces of Citron very fine, with ſix Ounces of fine Sugar: Beat the Yolks of nine Eggs to a Cream, and whiſk them together, with a Spoonful of the Juice of Spinage, and a little Brandy. Juſt as it is going in the Oven, put into it ſix Ounces of oiled Butter. Half an Hour bakes it. Keep it beating till it goes in the Oven.

To make a Rice Pudding.

WASH your Rice very well, and boil half a Pound in a Chopin of new Milk, till it is almoſt dry; then ſtir ſix Ounces of Butter in it, and let it cool a little; beat five Eggs, but three of the Whites, mix all together with a Gill of Cream, the Grate of an Orange or Lemon, a Quarter of a Pound of powdered Sugar, and a little Brandy. You may put Currants or Raiſins in it, if you pleaſe. Put Paſte about the Diſh, put a little beat Cinnamon and Nutmeg in it.

Another Way to make a Rice Pudding.

BOIL a Chopin of Milk, and thicken it with four large Spoonfuls of the Flour of Rice, blend the Rice in a little cold Cream or Milk, then ſtir it in your Milk on the Fire, with grated Lemon-peel and Nutmeg; ſweeten it to your Taſte, and when boiled pretty thick, take it off, and ſtir in it five Ounces of Butter; ſet it to cool, beat ſix Eggs, but three Whites, and when it is cold, mix them together, and put Paſte about the Diſh. You may make an Oat-meal Pudding the ſame Way: Put a little beat Cinnamon in them, and Nutmeg.

To make a Potatoe Pudding.

BOIL the large white Potatoes, peal and pound half a Pound of them very well, beat twelve Eggs, four Whites, very thick, and whiſk in them half a Pound of fine powdered Sugar, then your Potatoes, grated Nutmeg, and a large Glaſs of Brandy: Put half a Pound of oiled Butter in it. Juſt as it is going into the Oven, put Puff Paſte about the Diſh. It takes three Quarters of an Hour to bake it. You may make a Carot Pudding the ſame Way.

To

To make a Sagoe Pudding.

WASH and pick your Sagoe, put it to boil in a Chopin of Water: There must be half a Pound of Sagoe; boil it with the Rind of a Lemon, and a Stick of Cinnamon; when boiled pretty stiff, put in two Gills of white Wine, and a grated Nutmeg: Take it up, and when cold, put to it six Eggs, but three Whites, well beaten; sweeten it to your Taste, and put it in the Oven, not too hot: When the Paste is baked, it is enough. You may make a Millet Pudding the same Way; but there must be eight Eggs, and half the Whites in it.

To make an Apple Pudding.

BAKE or roast six or seven large Apples, skin and core them, then rub them through a Search with the Back of a Spoon, beat a Quarter of a Pound of Biscuit, and mix with it; then beat eight Eggs, but three Whites, and beat them all up very well together, with beat Cinnamon, the Grate of a Lemon, and a little Orange-flower Water; sweeten it to your Taste, and just as you are going to put it in the Oven, put into it four Ounces of clarified Butter. Put Puff Paste about it: A little bakes it.

To make a Goose-berry Pudding.

SCALD two Chopins of Goose-berries, and rub them through a Search with the Back of a Spoon: Pound six Ounces of Spunge Biscuits, and mix with them eight Eggs, but half the Whites, and half a Pound of fine powdered Sugar; then put in the rest with Orange-flower Water. A very little bakes it.

To make a Tansy Pudding.

BEAT ten Eggs, with eight Ounces of fine Sugar, then put in half a Mutchkin of Spinage Juice, a Mutchkin of Cream, a little Brandy and Nutmeg, eight Ounces of Spunge Biscuit, or white Bread grated fine, a little Juice of Tansy to your Taste; the Tansy must be pounded and shred; a Quarter of a Pound of blanched and

pounded

pounded Almonds; mix all these well together in a Stew-pan, with three Ounces of Butter; set it on the Fire, stirring it till it is hard, then put it in your Dish, and bake it. Strew Sugar and sliced Orange on it. You may make a Tansy without Almonds the same Way.

To make a Marrow Pudding.

LAY thin Slices of Bread on your Dish, then lay on your Marrow in Lumps, then strew on Currants, so fill your Dish or Pudding-pan with Lairs; put a little beat Cinnamon, Nutmeg and Mace between the Lairs; beat eight Eggs, but two Whites, and a Chopin of Milk sweetened to your Taste; cover it. You may bake it without a Cover, if you please.

To make an Oat-meal Pudding.

BOIL a Quart of Water, season it with Sugar, Salt, Brandy and Nutmeg; thicken it with Oat-meal, till you can hardly stir the Spoon in it; add to it half a Pound of Currants, butter your Pan very thick. Pour it in, and half an Hour bakes it.

To make a Four-hour Pudding.

STONE and mince a Pound of Raisins; wash and pick a Pound of Currants; mince a Pound of Beef Sewet very fine; beat eight Eggs with four Spoonfuls of Flour, a Gill of Brandy, a little Bit of Cinnamon, and Nutmeg; stir them all together, butter your Bag, and tye it up very close; leave no Room, for it will not swell: You must boil it four Hours. The Sauce is Butter and Wine.

To make a Bread Pudding.

CUT all the soft of a Penny Loaf; boil a Mutchkin of Milk with a Stick of Cinnamon, and the Rind of a Lemon, and pour it on your Bread; your Bread must be cut in thin Slices; cover it up close for half an Hour; beat six Eggs, a little Sugar, a Glass of Brandy

and

and Nutmeg; mix all with your Bread: You may put in Currants, and a little Beef Sewet, if you please; butter your Bag, and tye it up very closs; an Hour and an half boils it; an Hour, if there is not Sewet and Currants in it.

To make a Flour Pudding.

BEAT eight Eggs, and mix in it three Spoonfuls of Flour, the Grate of a Lemon, Nutmeg, Sugar, a Glass of Brandy, a little Salt, and a Mutchkin of Milk; butter and flour your Cloth; tye it up closs, it takes three Quarters of an Hour to boil; let it, and all Puddings that are boiled, be put in boiling Water, and the Boil never given over till you send them up: Melted Butter and Wine is the best Sauce for these Puddings. Keep them stirring in the Pot as they are boiling.

A boiled Rice Pudding.

TAKE half a Pound of Rice, tye it loose in a Cloth, and boil it half an Hour; then add to it a good Piece of Butter, a little Cinnamon, Sugar, Salt, and the Grate of a Lemon; stir all together, and tye it up very closs; then boil it for an Hour. White Wine and Butter is the Sauce.

To make a Sewet Pudding.

SHREAD a Pound of Sewet very fine, a Pound of Flour, a Pound of Currants, six Eggs, a little Ginger, Nutmeg, Sugar, and Brandy; mix all together. Boil it three Hours.

To make an Oat-meal Pudding.

GET a Mutchkin of coarse Oat-meal, a Pound of Sewet shred small, half a Pound of Currants; season it with Sugar, Salt, Nutmeg, Mace, and the Grate of a Lemon; beat four Eggs and add to it; put it in your Cloth, and leave Room for it to swell. Two Hours will boil it.

To

To make a Custard Pudding.

BOIL a Mutchkin of Cream, with a Stick of Cinnamon, and the Rind of a Lemon and Orange; Sweeten it to your Taste; beat the Yolks of eight Eggs, and mix your Cream in them by Degrees; butter a white Stone Bowl, and put it in it; then butter a thick Piece of Cloth, and tye it on the Bottom of the Bowl; turn the Top down in boiling Water half an Hour; boil it, and tye it very fast.

An Orange Custards, or Pudding.

RUB the Out-side of four *Seville* Oranges with Salt, then pare them; lay the Peel in Water till the Bitterness is off them; then pound them very fine, and put in the Yolks of ten Eggs, and a Chopin of Cream; mix them well, and sweeten them to your Taste; put half a Pound of clarified Butter in it, if you bake it for a Pudding, and Puff Paste about the Dish; but if for Custards, put no Butter in, but put it in Cups. They both are to be baken.

To make a Lemon Pudding.

GRATE the Rind of three clear Lemons; put it to steep in Brandy; then grate two *Naples*, or Spunge Biscuits, and mix with it; beat the Yolks of ten Eggs and two of the Whites, and pound eight Ounces of Sugar very fine, and with the Eggs put in the Biscuits, the Rind of the Lemon, and Brandy, keeping it beating all the while; put Puff Paste about the Dish, and just as you are going to put it in the Dish, beat in half a Pound of clarified Butter. The Butter must be almost cold.

A Carot Pudding.

BOIL as many good Carots as will be half a Pound; cut them and pound them fine with half a Pound of fine Sugar; then beat ten Eggs and three Whites, and mix them with the Carots; grate an Orange in it, and just as you are going to put it into the Oven,

Oven, put into it half a Pound of clarified Butter. All the Butter that is put in baked Puddings must be clarified, and the Skim and Bottom taken from it.

A Yellow Pudding.

GRATE the Crumbs of a fine Two-penny Loaf, and put it in a Pudding Dish, and pour on it three Mutchkins of Milk, or Cream, five or six Eggs, a Pound of Beef Sewet, half a Pound of Raisins, and a Pound of Currants, some Saffron steeped in Rose Water, and strained into it; sweeten it to your Taste, and bake it. Pour the Milk on the Bread boiling hot.

To make a Barley Pudding.

PUT to a Quart of Cream, or Milk, the Yolks of six Eggs, and three Whites; beat them well; season it with Nutmeg, Salt, a little Orange-flower Water, and the Grate of an Orange and Lemon; then put in six Handfuls of Pearl Barley, but boil it a little in Milk first; put in it twelve Ounces of melted Butter; mix all together, with six Ounces of Sugar; butter a Dish, and pour it in. It takes a good while to bake it.

To make a boiled Apple Pudding.

MAKE a good Puff Paste, roll it out half an Inch thick; pare the Apples, and score them; fill the Paste and close it up; tye it in a Cloth, and boil it two Hours, if a large one three, then turn it out into the Dish; cut a Piece out of the Top of the Paste, and put Butter and Sugar in it to your Taste; then lay on the Piece again. A Pear, Damsons, or any Sort of Plumbs, Apricock, Cherries, Raspberries, Currants, Goose-berries, or Mulberry Puddings may be made the same Way. Send beat Butter, a little white Wine, and Sugar in a Bowl.

To make an Orange Pudding.

BOIL the Skins of three Oranges very tender; pound them very fine in a Marble or wooden Mortar; pound half a Pound of fine Sugar, and beat the Yolks of twelve Eggs to a Cream; mix your Sugar in them, then your Orange, beat them very well together; have eight Ounces of Butter melted to Oil, ſkim and bottom it; let it be as cold that it will but juſt pour before you put it in, and don't put it in till you are putting the Pudding in the Oven; put Puff Paſte about the Diſh, wipe it up before you put it in the Diſh; half an Hour bakes it. You muſt oil, ſkim and bottom all your Butter for baked Puddings, and let it be almoſt cold before you put it in.

To make a Lemon Pudding.

GRATE the Rind of four Lemons, and put it in a Glaſs of Brandy; beat the Yolks of ten Eggs till they are very thick, and pound and ſift half a Pound of Sugar, and beat it up well with your Eggs, then put in the Lemon Rind, and juſt as it is going into the Oven, put in eight Ounces of Butter, as above; put Puff Paſte about the Diſh of all baked Puddings. Half an Hour bakes it. Boil two Lemon Skins, and pound and mix them with this.

To make a Pudding of whole Rice.

PUT half a Pound of cold Butter on the Bottom of your Pudding-pan; ſtrew over it ſix Ounces of Rice, then half a Pound of Raiſins, or Currants, a grated Nutmeg; put over it two Chopins of new Milk: You may colour it with Saffron, it both eats and looks the better; grate the Rind of a Lemon, or Orange in it; don't ſtir it, but put it in a very hot Oven: It takes two Hours to bake it; ſweeten it to your Taſte; always ſtone the Raiſins, waſh, dry and pick the Currants, and waſh and dry your Rice.

To

To make Clary Cake.

BEAT ſix Eggs very well with Salt and Nutmeg; ſhread a Handful of Clary, and mix with them; fry them, or put it in a Diſh in the Dripping-pan when Meat is roaſting, and it will bake. You may make one the ſame Way with Chives and Parſley.

To make Pancakes.

BEAT ſix Eggs, and thicken them well with Flour, a little Ginger and Nutmeg, a little Salt, Sugar, and a Glaſs of Brandy; put to them a Mutchkin of Milk; fry them in Butter, either thick or thin, as you like.

To make Cuſtard Pancakes.

BEAT eight Eggs; mix in them with four Spoonfuls of Flour, a Glaſs of Brandy, a little Ginger and Nutmeg, Sugar, and the Grate of a Lemon; put to them a Mutchkin of Cream, and a little melted Butter; they will not turn in the Pan, but you muſt hold the upper Side to the Fire till criſp.

To make Pancakes.

BEAT four Eggs, a little Ginger, Nutmeg, and Salt; make them thick with Flour, then put in a Mutchkin of Two-penny; fry them criſp, and then you may put in Sugar, if you pleaſe.

To make Apple Dumplins.

MAKE Puff Paſte not too rich, and pare and ſcoop out the Cores of as many large Apples as will fill your Diſh at the black End; then put in the Place where you ſcoop out the Core, Currant Jelly or Marmalade of Oranges; roll out your Paſte thin, and roll up the Apples in it ſeparately; tye them up in Pieces of Cloth, and put them in a Pot of boiling Water: An Hour and a half boils them. Melted Butter, white Wine, and Sugar, is the proper Sauce.

To make fried Pan Puddings.

TO a Mutchkin of Milk put three Quarters of a Pound of Flour, ſix Ounces of Beef Sewet ſhred as fine as Flour, ſix Ounces of Currants waſhed and plumped, a little Salt, Nutmeg, a Glaſs of Brandy, and three or four Eggs; mix all well together; fry them in a Pan of Fat, and make them a little larger than Fritters.

Pancakes.

TAKE five Eggs, beat them very well with ſix Spoonfuls of Flour, the Grate of a Lemon, a little Ginger and Salt, and a Mutchkin of Milk; fry them very criſp, and then ſtrew Sugar on them, and ſend them in very hot.

To make French *Fritters.*

TAKE two Gills of Water, an Ounce of Butter, a little Cinnamon, Sugar and Brandy, and grated Lemon-peel; ſet it over the Fire, and boil the Water; ſtir in the Flour as faſt as you can, till in a Paſte; work it till it is like Paſte for ten Minutes; put it in a Bowl, work it with the Yolks of ſix Eggs and one White, till it is in a light Paſte; drop them in a Pan of boiling Fat, with a Spoon or a Knife; fry them a light brown, diſh them, and throw Sugar on them.

To make Apple Fritters.

BEAT four Eggs, make them pretty thick with Flour; put two Gills of Milk, a little Salt, Sugar, and Nutmeg into it; it muſt be as thick that it will ſtick to the Apples; pare and cut them in thin Slices, and take out the Cores, but don't break the Slices; put them in the Batter, and have a good deal of boiling Beef-dripping, and drop them in one by one till your Pan is full; fry them a light brown; then take them out, and put in more till they are all done; ſtrew on them Sugar when you diſh them: Any Kitchen-

fee

fee that is ſweet and clean will fry them. All Fritters are fried the ſame Way.

To make Potatoe Fritters.

BOIL and pound ſix Potatoes; mix them with five Eggs well beaten, a Gill of Cream, a little Sugar, Nutmeg, the Grate of an Orange, two Ounces of oiled Butter, and a little Brandy; beat all well together, drop them in a Pan almoſt full of boiling Fat, and fry them a light brown. Strew Sugar on them when diſhed.

To make Currant Fritters.

BEAT four Eggs with ſix Spoonfuls of Flour, and a little Salt, Sugar, Nutmeg, Ginger, and the Grate of a Lemon; then put in it half a Mutchkin of Cream, a Dram, and a Quarter of a Pound of Currants waſhed, picked and dried; drop them by Spoonfuls in a Pan almoſt full of boiling Fat. Fry them a light brown.

To make Barm Dumplins.

MAKE a light Dough, as for Bread, with Barm, Flour, an Egg and Water; then boil a Panful of Water, and put the Dough in it, making it into little round Balls as big as an Egg; then flat them with your Hand, and put them in the boiling Water: Ten Minutes boils them: Take care they don't fall to the Bottom. Send them to the Table with beat Butter in a Cup. Put Salt in them.

To make Hard Dumplins.

MIX Flour and Water, an Egg, and a little Salt, like a Paſte; roll them as before, then boil them in boiling Water for half an Hour: They are beſt boiled with Beef. Send Butter in a Cup with them.

Another Way to make Apple Dumplins.

PARE and core your Apples, and cut them in ſmall Pieces; then pare and core a Quince, and grate it among the Apples; then make a good Puff Paſte; roll it it in ſmall Pieces, and put in the Apples and Quinces; faſten them up and tye them in different Places in a a Cloth, and boil them; and when they are enough, take them out of the Cloth; cut a Bit out of the Top, and put in them Sugar and Butter, then diſh them, and put the Tops on them again.

A Florendine of Oranges, or Apples.

CUT half a Dozen *Seville* Oranges into Slices, and ſave the Juice; take out the Pulp, and lay them in Water twelve Hours; then boil them in Water till they are tender, keeping the Pan full of Water all the Time; then boil all the Juice, with a Pound of Sugar, and the Oranges cut in thin Slices; then boil ten Pipins in Water and Sugar; put them in the Diſh, and half the Oranges among them; cover it with a Lid of carved Puff Paſte. A Florendine of Currants is made the ſame Way.

An Almond Florendine.

BLANCH and beat very fine a Pound of Almonds with Orange-flower Water; beat eight Eggs, but half of the Whites; mix them with two Gills of Cream, and half a Gill of Brandy, half a Pound of clarified Butter, a Pound of Currants well waſhed and picked; ſeaſon it with Sugar, Cinnamon, and Nutmeg, all pounded fine; mix them all very well; put them in a Diſh with Puff Paſte under and over them: You may put candied Lemon, and Citron in thin Slices in it, if you pleaſe. A little while bakes it.

To make a plain Tanſy.

TAKE a fine ſtale Penny Loaf, and cut the Crumb in thin Shaves; put it in a Bowl, then boil a Mutchkin of Cream, and when boiled, pour it over the Bread, then cover the Bowl with a Plate, and let it ly a Quarter of an Hour; then mix it with eight Eggs well beaten, two Gills of the Juice of Spinage, two Spoonfuls of the Juice of Tanſy, and ſweeten it with Sugar, Nutmeg, and a little Brandy; rub your Pan with Butter, and put it in it; then keep it ſtirring on the Fire till it is pretty thick; then put it in a buttered Diſh; you may either bake it, or do it in the Dripping-Pan under roaſted Meat.

To boil a Tanſy.

CUT the Bread, as in the other Tanſy, and pour a Mutchkin of boiling Milk on it, cover it up, then beat eight Eggs with a little of the Grate of a Lemon or Orange, Nutmeg and Sugar; put to it ſome Juice of Spinage, and a little Tanſy Juice; ſtir all well together, then tye it up in a Cloth, and boil it an Hour and an Half; when you diſh it ſtick it with candied Orange, and cut a *Seville* Orange in Quarters round it; ſend beat Butter, white Wine and Sugar in a Cup with it to the Table.

A Pipin Tanſy.

PARE and cut as many Pipins as will cover the Bottom of a Diſh, then take half a Penny Loaf, crumb it fine, pour on it a Mutchkin of Cream, and eight Eggs well beaten; ſeaſon it with Sugar, Nutmeg and Ginger; put in a Gill of Spinage Juice, and a Spoonful of Tanſy Juice; beat all together, then put in your Slices of Apples, butter your Frying-pan, and put in the Tanſy; when the Pan is hot, you muſt fry it on both Sides, or you may bake it in the Oven; ſend beat Butter, Orange and Sugar to Table with it.

To make a White Pot.

TAKE two Chopins of Milk, mix with it nine Eggs well beaten, a little Roſe Water, grated Lemon-peel, Nutmeg, and Sugar; cut the Crumb of a Penny Loaf in thin Slices, and lay them in a Pudding-pan, then pour the Milk over them. You muſt put a little Butter on the Top. Put it in a ſlow Oven. Half an Hour bakes it.

Another

Another Sort of White Pot.

LAY a Lair of Marrow on the Bottom of the Dish you intend to bake it in, then lay all over it Slices of fine Bread cut very thin; strew over the Bread ston'd Raisins, putting grated Lemon-peel, Nutmeg and Ginger between them; then take a Chopin of Cream, and seven or eight Eggs well beaten, with Sugar, and a little Nutmeg; mix them with the Cream, and pour it over them softly, till the Dish is full: Let it stand a while before you put it in the Oven: Lay Slices of Bread, and Bits of Butter on the Top of all. You may make it with Currants, if you please.

A Rice White Pot.

BOIL a Chopin of Cream or Milk, then put in two Ounces of pick'd Rice, Sugar, Ginger, Cinnamon and Mace beaten; set it by to cool, beat six Yolks of Eggs, and two Whites, and mix them with the Cream; then put in four Ounces of pick'd and washed Currants, and a little Salt. You may bake it with or without Paste, boil the Rice a little, or put the Powder of Rice in it, instead of whole Rice.

Pancakes Royal.

MIX two Gills of Cream with two Gills of Sack, then beat up twelve Eggs, with Sugar, Cinnamon, Nutmeg and Ginger; mix them with as much Flour as will let them turn, then put in the Cream, and fry them with clarified Butter. The Pan must be always hot before you fry Pancakes.

Common Pancakes.

TAKE a Chopin of Milk, eight Spoonfuls of Flour, grated Nutmeg and Ginger; beat all together with a Glass of Brandy; let it stand a while, then fry them, and send them in hot with Sugar and Oranges.

Irish *Pancakes.*

BOIL a Mutchkin of Cream, with the Rind of an Orange, and some Cinnamon; then set it to cool: Beat eight Eggs, and but four of the Whites, with Sugar, Nutmeg, a little Salt, and two Gills of Flour; then beat three Ounces of sweet Butter, and mix the Cream and Eggs together, with a Glass of Brandy: Put a very little Bit of Butter in the Frying-pan, and when it is hot, put in two Gills of the Batter: They will not turn, but you must hold them before the Fire, to brown the upper Side.

To make Rice Pancakes.

BOIL a Chopin of Cream, thicken it with three Spoonfuls of the Flour of Rice, stir in half a Pound of Butter, and a grated Nutmeg; put it to cool, then beat eight Eggs and mix with the Cream; put in a little Salt, and sweeten it to your Taste; mix them well, and fry them in Butter; serve them up hot; if they don't fry well, put in a Spoonful of Flour.

Oat-meal Pancakes.

BOIL a Chopin of Milk, and blend in it a Mutchkin of the Flour of Oat-meal, thus: Keep a little Milk, and mix the Meal by Degrees in it, then stir in the boiling Milk; when it is pretty thick, put it to cool, then beat up six Eggs with Sugar, Nutmeg, the Grate of a Lemon, and a little Salt: Stir all together, and fry them in Butter, putting in a Spoonful of the Batter at a Time. Serve them up hot, with beat Butter, Orange and Sugar.

Chopped Apples in small Pancakes.

TAKE a Mutchkin of Milk, sweeten it to your Taste, then beat six Eggs, with Nutmeg, and the Grate of Lemon-peel; mix them with five or six Spoonfuls of Flour; then put in the Milk by Degrees, a Glass of Brandy, a little Salt, and Ginger; beat them up well, then

then put in chopped Apples. It muſt be pretty thick with them, then fry them in ſmall Pancakes.

To make criſp Pancakes.

TAKE four Eggs with Ginger and Salt, mix in them ſix or ſeven Spoonfuls of Flour, and a Mutchkin of Two-penny. You may put Lemon-peel and Nutmeg in them; fry them very thin in Butter: When you fry them firſt, if there is not enough of Flour, put in a little more.

To make a Clary Amulet.

BEAT eight or ten Eggs, with a little Pepper, Salt and Nutmeg; then put into it two Gills of Cream, and a Handful of Clary chopped very fine: Mix them well together, put ſome Butter or Beef-drippings in your Frying-pan, and when it is boiling hot, pour in your Amulet; fry it on both Sides, and ſend it up hot. You may make one of Parſley and Chives the ſame Way.

To poach Eggs and Spinage.

BOIL the Spinage in Water and Salt; chop them very ſmall, then ſqueeze them between two Trenchers, and mix them with a good Piece of ſweet Butter; ſalt them to your Taſte, then poach ſix or ſeven Eggs in boiling Water and Salt, letting the Water boil before you break in the Eggs; place the Spinage in an Aſhet, then lay the Eggs over them; take them up with an Egg-ſpoon, and don't break them; poach Eggs for Gravy the ſame Way; pour the Gravy ſcalding hot in the Diſh, and lay your poached Eggs in it.

Eggs with Cabbage Lettice.

SCALD ſome Cabbage Lettice in Water; ſqueeze them well, then ſlice them and toſs them up in Butter, with a little Gravy; ſeaſon it with Pepper and Salt, then let them ſtew for half an Hour on a ſlow Fire, being cloſe covered; then poach Eggs, and lay over them;

them when they are dished: You may put Sausages in the Dish round them.

To butter Eggs.

TAKE eight Eggs; put them in a Stew-pan after they are well beaten with a little Salt and Nutmeg; put to them a Quarter of a Pound of sweet Butter, and a Spoonful of sweet Cream, keep them stirring all the Time they are on the Fire from the Bottom of the Pan, then put them on toasted Bread when they are thick.

Fried Bacon and Eggs.

CUT thin Slices of Bacon and fry them a light brown; then take them up and clean the Pan; cover them; put a little Butter in the Pan, when it is clarified, break into it your Eggs; when they are a light brown, hold the Pan before the Fire to harden the other Side, for they must not be turned: Put the Bacon in the Dish, and the Eggs over them.

To make an Amulet.

GET what Quantity of Eggs you think will fill the Dish; season them with Pepper and Salt; ten Eggs will fill a small Dish; shread Parsley and Chives, and beat them and the Eggs with a Gill of Cream very well; then fry them in a Pan of good clarified Butter or Beef-dripping on both Sides: You may put in Gravy instead of Cream: You may put cut Slices of Oranges over it in the Dish.

Eggs and the Juice of Sorrel.

POACH your Eggs in Water, and have some Sorrel pounded; put the Juice of it in a Dish with some Butter, two or three raw Eggs, and Salt and Nutmeg; make all in a Sauce, and pour it on your poached Eggs. So serve them up.

A pretty Dish of Whites of Eggs.

TAKE the Whites of twelve Eggs, beat them up with four Spoonfuls of Rose Water, a little grated Lemon-peel, Nutmeg and Sugar; mix them well, and boil them in four small Bladders; tye them in the Shape of an Egg, and boil them hard, they will take half an Hour; lay them in the Dish, when they are cold mix two Gills of Cream with half a Gill of Malaga, a little Orange-juice and Sugar; then take out the Eggs, and pour the Cream over them in the Dish.

Eggs poached in Cream.

FILL a Dish almost full of Cream; put it on the Fire, and when the Cream boils, break as many Eggs in it as the Dish will hold; season it with Pepper, Salt, and Nutmeg; cover them with another Dish, but take care they are not too hard. Then serve them up.

Oisters or Cockles fried with Eggs.

WASH them well in their own Liquor; give them a Scald, let them cool; then beat ten or twelve Eggs, and mix them with Crumbs of Bread, Pepper, Nutmeg, and Salt; put in a Gill of Cream; beat them well, then put in your Oisters or Cockles; have the Pan with clarified Butter, then drop them in; turn them, and fry them a light brown: When one Panful is done, put more, so do till they are done. You may send Butter and Lemon-juice in a Cup, or Gravy. They are very pretty to garnish any Dish of Fish.

To make Puff Paste.

TO two Pound of Flour, you must have a Pound of Butter; rub in the Flour two Ounces of the Butter, and put in it two Eggs; then wet it cold, wet as much as will make a stiff Paste; work it very smooth, then roll out the Paste, and stick it all over with Butter; shake Flour on it, then roll it like a Collar, double it up at both Ends, that they meet in the Middle: Roll it out

out the ſame Way, and put it up as before, till all the Butter is in it.

Paſte for any raiſed Pies.

TO half a Peck of Flour, take two Pound of Butter; boil it in a Chopin of Water, make a Hole in the Flour, and pour in the Butter and Water; don't let the Sediment at the Bottom go in: Skim it clean, then work it up to a Paſte, and before it is quite cold, raiſe it up into any Shape you pleaſe, either ſmall or great Pies; if the Paſte is not wet enough, boil Water, and put in it. Do the ſame in all ſtanding Paſte.

Another Sort of Paſte.

TAKE half a Peck of Flour, and boil a Pound of Butter, and half a Pound of render'd Mutton Sewet in a Chopin of Water; wet it with it, and work it well while it is hot; raiſe it into any Shape for Paſties or Pies you pleaſe; it ſtands better with the Sewet mixed with Butter, than all Butter, but let it be very ſweet.

A Paſte of Drippings.

TAKE a Pound and a half of Drippings, boil it in Water, and ſtrain it; then let it cool, and take off the Fat; ſcrape it, and boil it ſo for four or five Times, then work it well up into three Pounds of Flour, and wet it with cold Water till it is a Paſte. It will be a very good Pye Cruſt; or if you wet the Flour with it and boiling Water, it will make raiſed Pies, but you muſt raiſe it while it is very hot.

Cold Water Paſte for Paſties.

LAY down half a Peck of Flour, wet it with two Eggs and cold Water, work it in a Paſte, then roll it out, and put over it a Pound and a Quarter of Butter, and flour it; then roll it like a Collar, and roll it again: Do that five or ſix Times, till you ſee the Butter is well mixed

mixed with the Paste, then you may cover any Sort of Pies with it.

Paste for Tarts.

TAKE a Pound of Flour, and rub it in a Quarter of a Pound of Butter, and a little fine Sugar; wet it with an Egg, and as much Water as will make it into Paste; then roll it into what Form you please for Tarts or Puddings.

To make Apple Tarts.

PARE two Oranges thin, and boil them in Water till they are tender; then shread them small, and pare twenty Pipins, quarter and core them, and put to them as much Water as will cover them; then put them on the Fire, and turn them softly, then put in half a Pound of Sugar, and the Orange-peel that was shred, and the Juice of the Orange, and let them boil till they are pretty thick; when they are cold, put them in your Crusts, with open Paste over them; glaze them with the White of an Egg, and grated Sugar, then bake them a light brown.

Goose-berry Tarts.

PUT Paste in the Patties, and give the Goose-berries a Scald; when they are cold, put them in the Patties, with Sugar under and over them; cover them with nicked Paste, and glaze them as before. Bake them in a slow Oven.

Prune Tarts.

STEW a Pound of Prunes, with a little Sugar and Water; stone some of them, and put in some of them without stoning; put Puff Paste under them and over them, with a little of the Liquor they were stewed in, so bake them. Glaze all Tarts as in the first Receipt of Tarts. You may stew the Prunes in Claret, if you please.

Chesnut

Chesnut Tarts.

ROAST the Chesnuts, peel them, and put Paste in the Patties; then put in your Chesnuts, and between every two Chesnuts, put a Bit of Marrow rolled in Eggs, and some Orange and Lemon-peel cut small; then make a Custard, and put it over them; bake them a little, then send them up hot or cold.

To make Sweet-meat Tarts.

PUT Puff Paste in the Bottom of the Patties, then put into them any Sort of preserv'd Fruit, then cut Paste in any Shape you please, or cross bar them; then glaze them, and put them in a slow Oven for a Quarter of an Hour. When the Paste is done, they are enough.

To keep Goose-berries for Tarts.

TAKE the Goose-berries before they are full grown, but come to their Taste; pick them off the Stems, then put them in Bottles that are very clean and dry, cork them very close, put them in a slow Oven, and when they turn white they are enough; then rosin the Corks, and keep them in Sand: When you are going to use them, boil them in a Syrup, and when they are cold put them in Puff Paste, and cut Holes in the Top; bake them in a slow Oven. You may keep red and black Currants the same Way.

Peach Tarts.

TAKE half ripe Peaches and pare them, and slice them in two, and take out the Stones, put some fine powdered Sugar in the Bottom of a Stew-pan, place your Peaches in it, put them over the Fire, and stir them often, then put Paste in the Patty-pans; and when the Peaches are cold put them in the Patties with the Syrup they were boiled in, cover them with rich Paste, and bake them in a slow Oven; put the Kernels of the Peaches in the Tarts. You may do Apricocks the same Way.

Raspberry Tarts.

PUT Paste in the Patties, then lay in the Raspberries, strew over them some fine Sugar; cover and bake them in a slow Oven: When they are cold you may put Cream on them. You may make Tarts the same Way of all Sorts of Fruit, but put a carved Paste Lid on them.

To make Orange Tarts.

BOIL the Skins of two bitter Oranges in four or five Waters, till all the Bitterness is off them, and the Skin is so tender that you may thrust a Straw in them; then drain them, and pound them and six Ounces of fine Sugar into a Paste, with some of the Juice of the Oranges, and some Pipins shred small; mix it all together, and put it into your Patty-pans with Paste under them, and cross Bars over them; put them in the Oven, half an Hour bakes them. You may make Lemon Tarts the same Way.

To make Orange Cheese-cakes.

BOIL the Skins of three Oranges in five or six Waters till the Bitterness is off them, then pound them very fine, with half a Pound of fine Sugar; beat the Yolks of eight Eggs and two Whites, till they are very thick and white; then mix the Oranges with them, and eight Ounces of oiled Butter: Put Paste in the Patty-pans, and half fill them; half an Hour bakes them in a slow Oven. Lemon Cheese-cakes are made the same Way; but you need not shift the Water they are boiled in, and put the Grate of an Orange or Lemon in them: Put a little Brandy in both.

To make Cheese-cakes.

TAKE two Chopins of Cream, or good Milk, and the Yolks of three Eggs, and four of the Whites, beat them very well; mix them with the Milk, and set it on the Fire, when it boils take it off and drain the Whey gently from it; put to the Curd grated Nutmeg, beat

beat Cinnamon, and three Spoonfuls of Rose-water, as much Malaga, some fine Sugar, four Ounces of Butter, a Quarter of pounded Biscuits, and a Quarter of Currants, pick and wash them; but before you put them in, blend all the rest very well together, then mix them in. You may bake them in any Shape or Crust you please.

To make Potatoe Cheese-cakes.

BOIL and peel the Potatoes, and pound six Ounces of them, then beat five Eggs, but three of the Whites, and mix the Potatoes with them, and four Ounces of Sugar, grated Lemon and Orange-peel, Nutmeg, and a Glass of Brandy; then, a little before you put them in the Patties, put in four Ounces of oil'd Butter almost cold. Put Puff Paste in the Patties under them.

To make Egg Cheese-cakes.

BEAT two Eggs well, and thicken them with Flour, then beat three Eggs, and mix them with a Mutchkin of Cream and six Ounces of Butter, put it on the Fire, and keep it stirring one Way; when it is almost boiling put in the two Eggs and Flour, keep it stirring, and when it is boiled pretty thick, take it off the Fire, and season it with Sugar, Salt, grated Lemon-peel, and Nutmeg; when they are cold put in half a Pound of Currants wash'd, pick'd and dried; put Paste in your Patties, and bake them half an Hour.

To make Almond Cheese-cakes.

TAKE half a Pound of Almonds, blanch and pound them, keeping them wetting with Brandy, or Rose-water; beat five Eggs, but one White, mix them and your Almonds with six Ounces of fine Sugar, the Grate of two Oranges or Lemon-peel, six Ounces of Butter oil'd, skim and bottom it; then just as they are going into the Oven put in the Butter, beat all well together, put Puff Paste in the Patties, put a little Brandy in them, then

then put them in the Oven. Half an Hour bakes them.

To make Almond Custards.

BOIL a Mutchkin of Cream with Cinnamon, and Orange or Lemon-peel in it; beat the Yolks of seven Eggs, and mix them with a little of the Cream before you boil it; then mix all together, with a Quarter of a Pound of Almonds blanched and pounded, and a little Orange-flower Water; sweeten them to your Taste; put them on the Fire again, and keep it stirring one Way till it is almost boiling; then take it up, and put it in Cups; take out the Cinnamon and Peel: You may put the Cups in the Oven to colour them, or you may send them to Table as they are. Grate Nutmeg on them.

To make Custards of Rice.

BOIL a Mutchkin of Milk with two Ounces of fresh Butter in it; keep out a little of the Milk, and stir in it two Spoonfuls of the Powder of Rice, and two Eggs well beaten; then mix them with the boiled Milk; put in a Spoonful of Orange-flower or Rose-water; sweeten it to your Taste; put it on the Fire, and keep it stirring till it is pretty thick; boil the Rice in the Milk before you put in the Eggs, and don't let it boil after the Eggs go in, but let it be scalding hot.

To make Custards.

BEAT six Eggs very well, leave out four of the Whites; mix them with a Mutchkin of Milk, the Grate of a Lemon, and Nutmeg; sweeten it to your Taste; put it in Cups, and put them in a Stew-pan of cold Water on a slow Fire: Don't put as much Water in the Pan as will come over them; put it on a slow Fire; cover the Pan with the Lid, and when the Custards are stiff, take them out: You may brown them with a Salamander. You may do any Custards in Water the same Way.

Orange

Orange Custards.

TAKE the Juice of two *Seville* Oranges with a little of the Peel grated, and as much Sugar as will make it sweet; give it a Boil, and strain it, then boil a Mutchkin of Cream, with Nutmeg, Cinnamon, and Sugar; thicken it with the Whites of five or six Eggs beaten, then beat them all together, and put it in Cups.

Another Sort of Almond Custards.

BLANCH and pound a Handful of Almonds; then put to them a Mutchkin of Milk, press the Milk out, and sweeten it; then beat five Eggs, but two of the Whites, and mix them with the Milk; put it in Cups: You may put them in the Oven, or do them in a Pan with Water.

To put Sweet-meats of all Colours in Jelly.

LET your Jelly be very stiff, and season it and clear it as you do other Jelly; put a little in the Bottom of the Turks-cap; let it stand to cool, then lay it all over with different coloured whole Sweet-meats; then put on a little more Jelly, as much as will be half an Inch above the Sweet-meats; let it cool again, and lay on more, so go on till the Bowl is filled, but there must be an Inch of Jelly above all: When it is very cold, turn it out on an Ashet with the broad Part down.

To make a Trifle.

COVER your Ashet with Spunge Biscuits, then pour over them a Mutchkin of Malaga, or white Wine; then a yellow Cream; then lay on it Heaps of coloured Sweet-meats; roast six or seven Apples, and rub them through a Search; put a little Sugar to them, and mix them with four Eggs, the Whites only, and wipe them up very high, and put this by Spoonfuls over the rest; but let a little of the Cream and Sweet-meats be seen. Raise it up as high as you can, so send it to the Table.

To make Burnt Cream.

BOIL a Mutchkin of Cream, and thicken it with the Yolks of eight Eggs and a Spoonful of Flour; boil Cinnamon and the Rind of an Orange in the Cream; take care it is not curdled; sweeten it to your Taste; take a Quarter of a Pound of Loaf-sugar in a Stew-pan, and pour over it half a Gill of Water; let it boil till it ropes, and don't stir it till you take it off; then by Degrees strew it over your Ashet of Cream; brown it with a Salamander, or in the Oven.

To make Jelly of Hartshorn.

TAKE a Pound of Hartshorn, put it in a Tea Kettle with two Pints of Water, *Scots* Measure, and a Penny-worth of Isinglass; let it boil on a very slow Fire to a Pint; then strain it off and set it to cool; if it is too stiff, put in a little Water, and if too limber, put in another Penny-worth of Isinglass, and boil it better; it takes a great deal of boiling more than any other Stock for Jelly; season it with white Wine, Sugar, Lemons, and Cinnamon to your Taste; put the Rind of a Lemon in it; beat the Whites of six Eggs, and whisk them in it: You must keep it stirring all the while it is on the Fire; have a thin Cloth tied on the Bottom of a Chair or Frame; boil it a Quarter of an Hour, and pour it up boiling hot; change the Bowl till you see it is clear. So put it in Glasses for your Use.

To make Calves Feet Jelly.

SCALD the Hair off them very clean, then slit them into, and let them lye in warm Water two Hours; put them into a closs covered Sauce-pan with a Quarter of a Pound of Hartshorn, or Two-pence worth of Isinglass; put two Pints of Water to them, and let them boil very slow till they are all in Tavers; then put a little of the Stock to cool, and if it is stiff, strain it off; skim it very clean, and let it stand to settle; leave all the Settling at the Bottom; if it is too stiff put in a little Water, if not, boil it better: The best Way to season

ſeaſon Jelly is to your Taſte, but you may put a Mutchkin of Wine and four Lemons to three Mutchkins of Stock; ſeaſon it with Cinnamon, Sugar, and the Rind of a Lemon; clear it as you do the Hartſhorn Jelly, with Whites of Eggs.

To make Blamong.

MAKE your Stock as you do for Jelly, but a great deal ſtiffer; to a Mutchkin of Stock put a Quarter of a Pound of Almonds blanched and pounded very fine, ſix bitter ones; as you are pounding wet them with a little Cream; boil Lemon-peel and Cinnamon in your Stock; ſweeten it to your Taſte, and when it is pretty warm, rub the Almonds in it very well thro' a Cloth; ſtrain it, and if it is not white enough, put in a Gill of thick ſweet Cream; put in a little Orange-flower Water, if you have it: You may put it either in Cups, or any Thing you pleaſe, it will turn out if cold enough. Wet the Cups with Cream.

To make Leech Cream.

TAKE a Quarter of a Pound of Iſinglaſs, pull it in Pieces, and put it to boil in a cloſs covered Sauce-pan, with three Mutchkins of Water; let it boil on a very ſlow Fire, till it is all diſſolved, and the half boiled away; put it to cool, and if it be ſtiff, put to it half a Mutchkin of Cream, the Rind of a Lemon and Orange, a Stick of Cinnamon, and ſweeten it to your Taſte. You may whiten it with pounded Almonds, if you pleaſe. It is a very pretty Supper Diſh; when quite cold, ſtick Bits of Marmalade of Oranges and Almonds cut like Straws in it. It is good for any one in a Decay.

To make whipt Sillabubs.

TAKE a Mutchkin of thick Cream, put to it half a Mutchkin of white Wine, the Juice of a Lemon, and grate the Rind in it; ſweeten it to your Taſte, whiſk it up well, ſkim off the Top as you are whiſking it, and put

put it on a Sieve; then put Wine in the Glass, either white or red, and a little Sugar; then send it to Table with Tea Spoons about it.

To make Orange Cream.

PARE the Rind of three bitter Oranges, and steep them in two Gills of Water, till it has a strong Flavour of the Orange; then squeeze the Juice in it, beat the Yolks of six Eggs, but first boil your Liquor with half a Pound of fine Sugar, then mix in your Eggs by Degrees, for Fear of curdling. Let it have a Scald on the Fire, stirring it one Way. Put it in Cups or Glasses, cutting some of the Orange-peel like Threads, and hang them about the Rim.

To make Lemon Cream.

LEMON Cream is made the same Way, but with more Sugar, and two more Whites of Eggs. You must not whip the Whites much, or they will froth, and not thicken: When you mix your Liquor and Eggs, you must strain it before you put it on the Fire. It must not boil, but be scalding hot, always stirring one Way. There must not be any Yolks of Eggs in this.

Maids Cream.

TAKE the Whites of five Eggs, and whisk them to a Froth, then put them in a Sauce-pan, with very fine Sugar, three Gills of Cream, a Spoonful of Orange-flower Water, and a little pounded Cinnamon: Put it on the Fire, and keep it stirring one Way all the Time. Don't let it boil, but it must be scalding hot; then put it in the Ashet, and brown it with a red hot Shovel.

To make a Rhenish Wine Cream.

PUT on the Fire a Mutchkin of Rhenish Wine, and a Stick of Cinnamon, and six Ounces of Loaf-sugar; while it is boiling, take six Eggs, whisk them very well, then whisk in the Wine by Degrees, then put it on the

Fire,

Fire, and keep it whiſking all the Time, till it is pretty thick. It muſt not boil after the Eggs are in. Boil the Rind of a Lemon or Orange in the Wine; keep it whiſking all the Time, and when it is ſcalding hot, take it off, and put it in Cups, with as high a Froth as you can whiſk on it. You may make any Sort of white Wine the ſame Way.

To make Currant Cream.

BOIL a Mutchkin of Cream, and thicken it with two Eggs; when it is cold, put to it the Juice of a Chopin of Currants, and put the Currants in a Pan on the Fire, maſh them, and when they are thoroughly hot, ſtrain out the Juice, and ſweeten it to your Taſte; then mix it with the Cream, and put it in Cups. You may do Raſp-berry or Straw-berry Cream the ſame Way. Don't let the Cream boil after you put in the Eggs at any Time, but it muſt be ſcalding hot.

Sack Cream.

TAKE a Chopin of Cream, put it on the Fire with the Rind of a Lemon, and when it boils, take it off; beat two Eggs, and mix the Cream with them by Degrees, ſtirring them all the Time; then put it on the Fire again, and when it is ſcalding hot, take it off, and ſtir it one Way all the Time it is on the Fire; then take the China Bowl that you ſerve it to Table in, and put the Juice of half a Lemon, and nine Spoonfuls of Sack in it, and ſweeten both the Cream and Sack; then put in the Cream in the Bowl by Spoonfuls; ſend it up when quite cold, and keep it ſtirring till almoſt cold.

To make yellow Lemon Cream.

GRATE off the Peel of four Lemons, ſqueeze the Juice to it, and let it ſtand five Hours, then ſtrain it, and put to it the Whites of eight Eggs, and two Yolks well beaten and ſtrained, a Pound of double refined Sugar, and a Gill of Roſe-water; ſtir it well and ſet it on on the Fire, keep it ſtirring one Way, don't let it boil, when it comes to Cream it is enough.

Yellow Cream.

BOIL a Mutchkin of Cream with a Stick of Cinnamon, and the Rind of an Orange, then beat up the Yolks of eight Eggs with Roſe-water, and when the Cream is almoſt cold mix the Eggs with it by Degrees, ſweeten it to your Taſte; put it on a ſlow Fire, and keep it ſtirring one Way, till it is ſcalding hot, don't let it boil, then pour it in a Bowl, keep it ſtirring for a while, then whip up the Whites of Eggs to a Snow, and put them in the Oven, or before the Fire to harden; pour the Cream in your Diſh, but take out the Orange-peel and Cinnamon; put red Currant-jelly, Marmalade of Oranges and any different coloured Sweet-meats about the Diſh, in Heaps, with the Whites of Eggs between every Heap. It is to be eaten cold.

Almond Cream.

BOIL a Chopin of Cream with Cinnamon, Lemon-peel and ſliced Nutmeg; then blanch and pound ſome Almonds with Roſe-water, then take the Whites of nine Eggs well beaten, and put them into your Almonds, then rub them very well through a fine Search, ſo thicken your Cream with them; keep it ſtirring on a ſlow Fire till it is ſcalding hot; ſweeten it to your Taſte, you may put it in a Diſh, or in Cups.

Ratafia Cream.

BOIL four Laurel Leaves in a Chopin of Cream, and beat up the Yolks of five Eggs in a little cold Cream, and mix it with the reſt, put it on the Fire, and keep it ſtirring one Way; don't let it boil, but be ſcalding hot: Then take out the Leaves and ſweeten it to your Taſte, then put it in Cups. It is to be eaten cold.

To

To make Steeple Cream.

BOIL a Chopin of Cream, with two Pints of Milk, set it to cool, and skim the Cream off it, then boil it again, and set it to cool; skim it, keep it boiling, and cooling and skimming till you have a Chopin of Cream that a Spoon will almost stand in it; take Care to stir it in the boiling, that no Brats come on it: Put in it, just as you are going to whisk it, half a Mutchkin of Malaga, a little fine Sugar, and the Juice of a Lemon; you must whisk it up very thick and raise it up on the Ashet in the Shape of a Sugar Loaf: Strew it all over with coloured confected Carraways, and garnish it with different coloured Sweet-meats.

To make Strawberry or Raspberry Cream.

MASH them small, and boil them with an equal Weight of Loaf-Sugar; when cold put to it a Mutchkin of Cream, or four or five Spoonfuls of either of them, and whisk them as you do Sillabubs. So fill your Glasses.

To make Coddlen or Goose-berry Cream.

CODDLE your Apples, till they are so soft that you will rub them thro' a Search with the Back of a Spoon, sweeten them to your Taste; when they are cold mix them with Cream: Goose-berries are done the same Way. Put them on an Ashet.

To make a very pretty red Cream.

TAKE a Mutchkin of Cream, and colour it with Cocheneal: Put the Grate of an Orange and Lemon in it, a little Malaga, and the White of an Egg; sweeten it to your Taste; whip it up thick and put it in Glasses. Any one may eat it, for Cocheneal is very wholesome.

To make Cream Deloutee.

TAKE a Mutchkin of Cream, the Rind of a Lemon or Orange-peel, and a Stick of Cinnamon, sweeten

ten it to your Taste; let it stand till it is almost as cold as new Milk, then take the yellow Skins that are in the Gizzards of two Fowls, wash them clean, cut them small, and put them in the Cream; then strain the Cream through a thin Clothinto the Ashet, rubbing the Cloth; strain it two or three times, still keeping it rubbing: You must be very quick in straining it, or it will jelly in the Cloth; then put it on warm Water, and cover the Ashet, then put Fire on the Cover; when it is jelly'd take it off gently, and set it to cool, then serve it up: It must be the Skins of the Gizzards of Hens, Chickens or Turkies.

To make Rice Cream.

TAKE three Spoonfuls of the Flour of Rice, three Yolks of Eggs, three Spoonfuls of Water, and two Spoonfuls of Orange-flower Water; mix them well together, and put to them a Mutchkin of Cream, and set it on the Fire; keep it stirring till of a right Thickness, then dish it and eat it cold.

Clouted Cream.

TAKE an *English* Gallon of good new Milk, scald it on a clear Fire, and keep it stirring when it is at the Boil; take it off and stir it a little, then put it in a Milk-pan; let it stand twenty four Hours, then divide the Cream with a Knife as it stands upon the Pan, and take it off with a Skimmer that the Milk may run from it; then lay it on a Dish, one Piece upon another, with fine Sugar between each Piece till the Dish is full; keep it thus twenty four Hours before you spread it: If you please beat Part of it with a little Rose-water, and a Lair of it, and a Lair of unbeaten Clouts, with Sugar between; this clouted Cream beaten with a Spoon till it is thick and light, makes *Spanish* Cream. It must be done with a little Rose-water and Sugar.

Sack

Sack Cream.

BOIL a Bottle of white Wine, a little Cinnamon and Sugar to your Taste; then beat four Eggs with a little Nutmeg, and mix in the Wine by Degrees, keeping the Eggs beating all the Time; then put it on the Fire and keep it whisking; don't let it boil, but scalding hot; put it in Candle Cups, send it hot to Table with a great Froth whisked on it; if you like it stiff and cold, put in the Yolks of eight Eggs, and two Whites.

To make Tablets.

WET a Pound of double refined Sugar, with two Gills of Water, it must be very finely pounded; put it on the Fire and keep it stirring all the Time till the Drop stands on the Spoon; and when it begins to candy about the Sides of the Pan, it is enough. Oil a Dish, and just as you are going to pour it out, put in it two Tea Spoonfuls of the Oil of Cinnamon, keeping it always stirring till you pour it on the Dish: When almost cold, cut it in any Shape you please. Ginger Tablets are made the same Way; but instead of the Oil of Cinnamon, put in two Drops of Ginger, beaten and sifted very fine.

To make a Crokain.

TAKE three Quarters of a Pound of fine Sugar, put it in a clear Copper-pan with two Gills of Water; put it on the Fire, let it boil slow, skim it, but don't stir it; put in the Juice of half a Lemon, then let it boil brown; then take a Spoon and try if it ropes; oil your Mold, and spin it on as neatly as you can, and let it be pretty thick at the Bottom; when it is done, take it off as gently as you can. You may put any of the Creams mentioned in this Book, or red or green preserved Apples or Oranges, under it.

To make a floating Island.

TAKE half a Pound of Currant Jelly, and the Whites of four Eggs; put them in a large Bowl, and whisk it till it is as thick that you may drop it with a Spoon into any Shape you please: You must keep whisking all one Way, it takes a long Time to whisk it; and it must be whisked from the Bottom of the Bowl; then drop it by Spoonfuls in an Ashet, and raise it up as high as you can; put under it two Gills of Cream, a Spoonful of Rose-water, and a little Sugar: You may make it of roasted Apples the same Way, but they must be cold, and mash them with the Back of a Spoon. You may put a yellow Cream under it, but don't make it too stiff.

Solid Sillabubs.

TAKE a Chopin of very thick Cream, put into it three Gills of Malaga, the Grate of a Lemon, the Juice of two bitter Oranges, and sweeten it to your Taste; beat it well together for a Quarter of an Hour, then skim it with a Spoon, and put it in Glasses.

To make Sillabubs from the Cow.

SWEETEN either Wine, Cedar, or strong Ale, put it in a Bowl, take it to the Cow, and milk her on your Liquor as fast as you can. You may make it at home, by warming it, and pour it on the Liquor out of a Tea Pot.

A Jelly Posset.

TAKE twelve Eggs, leave out half the Whites, and beat them very well, put them into a large Bowl or a Soup Dish, with a Mutchkin of Malaga or strong Ale; sweeten it to your Taste, and set it on a Pan or Pot of boiling Water, keeping it stirring all the Time; then have ready a Chopin of Milk or Cream, boiled with Cinnamon and Nutmeg, and when your Wine and Eggs are scalding hot, put the Milk to them boiling hot, then

take

take it off the Fire, and cover it for half an Hour, so send it up.

A Sack Posset, or what is called the Snow Posset.

BOIL a Chopin of Cream or Milk with Cinnamon and Nutmeg; then beat the Yolks of ten Eggs, and mix them with a little cold Milk; then by Degrees mix them with the Cream; stir it on the Fire till it is scalding hot; sweeten it to your Taste; put in your Dish a Mutchkin of Sack, with some Sugar and Nutmeg; set it on a Pot of boiling Water, and when the Wine is hot, let one take the Cream, and another the Whites of the Eggs, and pour them both in holding your Hands high, and stirring all together while it is on the Fire; when it is scalding hot, take it off, cover it, and let it stand a while before you send it to Table. The Whites must be beaten with a little Sack.

To make Oat-meal Flummery.

PUT three large Handfuls of Oat-meal ground small in two Chopins of Water: Let it steep a Day and a Night; then pour off the clear Water, and put two Chopins more on it, and let it stand the same Time, then stir it, and strain it through a Hair-sieve, till it is as Porridge, that is, what is called in *England* Hasty Pudding; stir it all the Time, that it may be extremely smooth before you set it on the Fire; put in a Spoonful of Sugar, and two of Orange-flower Water; when it is boiled enough, pour it in a shallow Dish; when cold, you may eat it with Wine and Sugar, Ale or Milk.

To make Scots *Flummery.*

TAKE a Mutchkin of Milk, and one of Cream; beat the Yolks of nine Eggs, with a little Rose-water, Sugar and Nutmeg; put it in a Dish, and the Dish over a Pan of boiling Water covered close; when it begins to grow thick, have ready some Currants plumped in Sack, and strew over it. It must not be stirred while it

is

is over the Fire, and when it is pretty stiff; send it up hot.

To make West Country Flummery.

LAY half a Peck of Wheat Brawn in Steep, in cold Water, for three or four Days; then strain it, and boil it to a Jelly; Sweeten it with Sugar, and put in either Orange-flower, or Rose-water; then set it to cool, and eat it with Cream, Milk, Wine or Beer.

To make a Hedge-hog.

BLANCH and beat a Pound of Almonds very fine, with a Spoonful of Sack or Orange-flower Water, to keep them from oiling; make it into a stiff Paste, then beat six Eggs, and put two Whites, sweeten it with fine Sugar, then put in half a Mutchkin of Cream and a Quarter of a Pound of beat Butter, set it on your Stove, and keep it stirring till it is stiff, that you make it into the Shape of a Hedge-hog, then stick it full of blanched Almonds cut in Straws; set them on it like the Bristles, with two Currants plump'd for Eyes; then place it in the Middle of the Dish, and boil some Cream; put in it the Yolks of two Eggs, and sweeten it to your Taste; put it on a slow Fire, and when it is scalding hot take it off; you must keep it stirring all the while; when it is cold put it about the Hedge-hog.

To make Flummery Caudle.

TAKE a Mutchkin of fine Oat-meal, put to it two Chopins of Water, let it stand twelve Hours; then strain it into a Skellet with a little Mace and Nutmeg; set it on the Fire and keep it stirring, and let it boil a Quarter of an Hour; if it is too thick put in more Water, and let it boil longer; add to it a Mutchkin of white Wine, the Juice of a Lemon or Orange, and a Bit of Butter: Sweeten it to your Taste; let it have one Boil. You may put in the Yolks of two Eggs, but let it boil after you put in the Eggs; let it be scalding hot, keep it stirring till you dish it.

To

To make Hartshorn Flummery.

TAKE a Mutchkin of very stiff Hartshorn Jelly, and put to it two Gills of Cream, Nutmeg, Cinnamon, Lemon-peel, and two Laurel Leaves, sweeten it to your Taste, boil all together in a clean Sauce-pan; then strain it in large Cups, and when cold turn it out in a Dish; put Cream, Sugar and Wine about them.

To make a Calf's Foot Flummery.

TAKE four Calf's Feet, split them, and take out the long Bone, put them in three Chopins of Water, with some Cinnamon, Mace, Nutmeg, and Lemon-peel, let it boil gently till it is a strong Jelly; set it to cool, and skim off all the Fat, but strain it first; when cold take the Sediment, put it in the Pan with a Mutchkin of Cream, sweeten it to your Taste, put it over the Fire; take the Yolks of eight Eggs and beat them very well, with a little cold Cream; when the Jelly is lukewarm put in the Eggs, keep it stirring till the Eggs begin to be set, sweeten it to your Taste; then run it through a Sieve, and put it in Cups. It is to be eaten cold.

A Sack or Ale Posset.

BOIL a Chopin of Cream, or new Milk, and grate in five or six fine Biscuits, and let them boil with the Cream, season it with Sugar and Nutmeg, let it stand a little to cool; then put half a Mutchkin of Sack or strong Ale in your Dish or Bowl: Let it be a little hot, then hold up your Hand pretty high, and pour in the Cream: Let it stand a little, then send it up.

A Sack Posset without Cream or Eggs.

TAKE a Pound of *Jordan* Almonds, lay them all Night in Water, then blanch and beat them very fine, with a Gill of Orange-flower Water, and put them in a Chopin of Water, with the Crumbs of a Penny Loaf, beat Cinnamon, Nutmeg and Sugar; let it boil till it be pretty thick, keep it stirring all the Time, then warm

two

two Gills of Sack and put to it, ſtir all together; ſerve it up hot.

A very good Poſſet.

TAKE a Chopin of Cream, and mix it with a Mutchkin of ſtrong Ale, then beat the Yolks of eight Eggs, and three of the Whites, then put them to the Cream and Ale; ſweeten it to your Taſte, and grate Nutmeg in it; ſet it over the Fire, and keep it ſtirring all the while; when it is thick, and before it boils, take it off, and put it in the Diſh very gently, ſo ſend it up; ſtir all Things but one Way that have Eggs in them.

To make an Oat-meal Poſſet.

TAKE a Mutchkin of Milk, boil it with Nutmeg and Cinnamon, and put in it two Spoonfuls of Flour of Oat-meal, and boil it till the Rawneſs is off the Oat-meal; then take three Spoonfuls of Sack, and three of Ale, and two of Sugar; ſet it over the Fire till it is ſcalding hot, then put them to the Milk, give it one Stir, and let it ſtand on the Fire a Minute or two, and pour it in your Bowl; cover it and let it ſtand a little, then ſend it up.

Egg Cheeſe.

TAKE a Chopin of Milk, a Mutchkin of Cream, beat, and ten Eggs; leave out four Whites, mix them well with the Cream, Lemon-peel, Cinnamon, Sugar, Roſe-water, and half a Mutchkin of white Wine; then ſet it on the Fire, and keep it ſtirring all the Time till it boils; when you ſee it broke, take it off and put it in any ſhaped Mold that has Holes in it, till the Whey runs out; when cold, put it on the Diſh: You may put Wine and Sugar on them, or you may boil two Gills of Cream, thicken it with the Yolks of two Eggs, and pour it about it.

Cheeſe Loaves.

TAKE three Chopins of Milk, put a Spoonful of Runnet in it; and when it is come, preſs the Whey gently

gently out of it; then put as much grated Bread as Curd, and the Yolks of twelve Eggs, six Whites, two Gills of Cream, beat Cinnamon, Mace, Nutmeg, Sugar, two Spoonfuls of Flour, a little Salt, and a Glass of Sack or Brandy; make it into a Paste, roll some of it thin to fry; make the rest in a Loaf, and bake it, then cut a Hole in the Top, pour in some beat Butter, Cream and Sugar; put the fried Cakes about it in the Dish, and send it up hot.

Almond Puffs.

BLANCH two Ounces of Almonds, then take their Weight of fine Loaf-sugar, beat them together with Orange-flower Water; then whip up the Whites of three Eggs and put to them, and add as much sifted Sugar as will make it into a Paste; then make it into little Cakes, and bake them in a very slow Oven.

Pudding Puffs.

TAKE half a Mutchkin of Cream and three well beaten Eggs, three Spoonfuls of Flour, two Spoonfuls of Rose-water, Sugar, Nutmeg, and a little Salt; mix all well together; butter some Cups, and fill them more than half full of it, and bake them ten Minutes in a slow Oven: When they are done, turn them out on a Dish, and grate Sugar on them; send them up hot.

Lemon Puffs.

BEAT and sift a Pound of Loaf-sugar, mix it with the Juice of two Lemons, and the Rind grated fine; whisk the Whites of three Eggs to a Snow; then beat all together very well; sift Sugar on Papers, and drop it on by Spoonfuls; don't let them be too near one another; put them in a very slow Oven. You may make Orange Puffs the same Way.

Orange Loaves.

CUT a Bit out of the End of the Oranges, and take out all the Inside, and grate them; boil them in different

different Waters till they are tender, and all the Bitterness off them; let them dry, and boil them in a thin Syrup, till it has penetrated through them very well; then let them stand in the Syrup a Day or two, then take the Yolks of six Eggs, two Whites, a Quarter of a Pound of fine Biscuits pounded, Butter, two Gills of Cream, some of the Grate of the Orange, Sugar and Nutmeg; put it in a Pan, and stir it on the Fire till it is thick, then stir in it a little Brandy, and fill the Orange Skins; bake and serve them up, with beat Butter, Wine, and Sugar in a Cup.

To make Wafers.

LET the Flour be very dry; make it in a thick Batter with Cream; season it with Sugar and Cinnamon, and a very little Salt; beat an Egg very well, and put in it; butter your Irons, and let them be very hot, then put in a Tea-spoonful of the Batter; clap the Irons together, and hold them on the Fire for half a Minute, turning them; then take out the Wafer, and give it a Turn round your Finger, till it is in the Shape of a Funnel; as fast as you make them lay them on a Dish before the Fire.

Dutch *Wafers.*

BEAT four Eggs very well, mix with them a Pound of Flour, a Mutchkin of Cream, twelve Ounces of beat Butter; season it with Sugar, Nutmeg, and Rose-water; put in two Spoonfuls of Barm, mix all well together, and bake them in your Wafer-irons; there must be more of the Batter put in these than the other Wafers, and they take a longer Time on the Fire.

To make a Hen's Nest.

TAKE Calves Feet Jelly that is very strong, and put it in a white Bowl, or a Turks-cap; fill it near half full of the Jelly, let it be cold; take five Eggs, make a Hole

in

in the narrow End of them, that the Yolks and Whites may come out; then fill them with Blamong: Let them ſtand till they are cold, then take off the Shells by Pieces, and take care not to break the Blamong; then lay them in the Middle of the Jelly, ſo that they don't touch one another; then pour more Jelly on them when it is almoſt cold: Cut ſome Lemon-peel as Straws, and when the Jelly is ſtiff, ſtrew it over it; then pour a little more Jelly over it: When all is cold and very ſtiff, dip the Bowl in hot Water; have an Aſhet ready, and put it on the Top of the Bowl, and turn it out quick: Don't let the Bowl be a Moment in the Water.

To make a Caudle for Sweet Pies.

TAKE two Gills of white Wine, a little Nutmeg, Sugar, and Lemon-peel; put it on the Fire, and when it is ſcalding hot, beat the Yolks of two Eggs, and mix them with a little cold Wine; then mix all together; keep it ſtirring till it is ſcalding hot, then take it up, and pour it over the Pye or Tart.

To make Fairy Butter.

TAKE the Yolks of four hard Eggs, and half a Pound of Loaf-ſugar beat and ſifted, half a Pound of freſh Butter; bray them in a clean Bowl with two Spoonfuls of Orange-flower Water; when it is well mixed, force it through a Corner of a thin Canvas Strainer in little Heaps on a Plate. It is a very pretty Supper Diſh.

To make a Slipcoat Cheeſe.

TAKE two *Engliſh* Gallons of hot Milk, juſt milked, and put to it twelve Spoonfuls of Runnet, and when it comes, put a thin Cloth in a Cheeſe-vat; then take out the Curd with a Saucer, and lay them as gently as you can; then pour a little Water ſoftly on the Curd, and let all the Whey run out; then put on more Curd and more Water; do this till the Vat is quite full, then put a Cloth over it, and a thin Board; and when it falls put more Curd to it, and lay a Pound Weight on the Board: This Quantity makes two Cheeſes; let it lye in the Vat ten Hours, then turn it with a dry Cloth, and put it in the Vat again, and let it ly ten Hours more; then turn it on a dry Board, and ſprinkle a little Salt on it; let it ly till the Salt is melted, then get Nettles, pluck off the Leaves and wipe them clean; ſpread them on a dry Board, and lay the Cheeſe on them; then cover it with them, and let it be kept in a warm Place: Change the Nettle Leaves twice a Day, wiping the Cheeſe every Time with a ſoft Cloth. It will be ripe in ten Days, or a Fortnight.

To make Cream Cheeſe, as at Newport.

GET a Vat, a Quarter and a half high, the Bottom and Top muſt not be faſtened, it muſt be four Square, with Holes all over; then take two Chopins of Cream, ſix Chopins of new Milk, and ſet it with Runnet; when it is come, put a dry Cloth in the Vat, and lay the Curd in it with a China Saucer, and put it into the Vat; ſtrew a little Salt in two or three Lairs till all the Curd is in; cover it and preſs it as other Cheeſes; let it ſtand two or three Days till all the Whey is out, but turn it with dry Cloths every Day; then ſalt it lightly two Days; let it dry without rubbing. It is to be made in *May*.

To make a good Cheeſe.

TAKE three Chopins of Milk hot from the Cow, and a Chopin of Cream; put one Spoonful of Runnet in it, and when it comes, break it and put in a little Salt; put a Cloth in the Vat, then put in the Curd, and preſs it as you do other Cheeſe; turn it in the Vat often, and when it is wheyed, ſalt it, then put it to dry, wiping and turning it every Day. You muſt not cut it till it is a Year old.

To

To make a thick Cheese.

TAKE the Milk of ten Cows, and put to it three Spoonfuls of Runnet, and when it comes, break it and whey it, and let it ly for a while; then whey it again, and when it is very well wheyed, break into it two Pounds of ſweet Butter, and a little Salt; then put it in the Vat, and preſs it very well; turn it very often, and change the Cloths: You may put wet Cloths at firſt about it, and thereafter put dry Cloths; let it ly fourteen Hours in the Preſs, then take it out and ſalt it a little; then dry it with a Cloth. Put it on a dry Board, and wipe and turn it every Day.

To make a Welſh *Rabbet.*

CUT Toaſts, and toaſt them on both Sides, then toaſt the Cheeſe on the Bread, and ſend it up hot.

To toaſt Cheeſe.

TOAST the Bread and ſock it in Wine, ſet it before the Fire, cut the Cheeſe in very thin Slices, rub Butter over the Bottom of a Plate, lay the Cheeſe in, pour in two or three Spoonfuls of Wine, cover it with another Plate, ſet it on a Chaffing-diſh of Coals for three Minutes; then mix it, and when it is done, lay it on the Bread; brown it with a Salamander, or a red hot Shovel.

To toaſt Cheeſe another Way.

TAKE a Quarter of a Pound of *Cheſhire* Cheeſe, not too fat, two Ounces of Butter, and two Eggs; beat all together very well, then prepare ſome Toaſts pretty brown; butter them on both Sides, then ſpread the Cheeſe upon them: Then brown it with a Salamander, or a red hot Fire-ſhovel. Serve it up hot.

To make Wigs.

TAKE a Quarter of a Peck of Flour, rub into it three Quarters of a Pound of Butter, ſomething more than

than Half a Pound of Sugar, a little Nutmeg and Ginger grated, three Eggs well beaten; put to them half a Mutchkin of thick Barm, and a Glaſs of Brandy, make a Hole in your Flour and pour all in, with as much warm Milk as will make it in a light Paſte; let it ſtand before the Fire to riſe half an Hour, then make it into a Dozen and a Half of Wigs. Bake them half an Hour.

A Plumb-cake or Bun.

TAKE five Pounds of Flour, and put to it half an Ounce of Nutmegs, Cloves and Mace, finely beaten, and a little Salt, mix all well together, then take a Chopin of Milk, let it boil, put into it three Pounds of Butter; when melted, and blood-warm, mix it with a Chopin of Barm, and two Gills of Brandy, twenty Eggs well beaten, ten Whites, ſix Pounds of well clean'd Currants; mix in the Flour, make a Hole in the Middle of your Flour, and put in the Milk and other Things, mixing it well with your Hands, cover it warm before the Fire to riſe; then put it in the Hoop, if the Oven is hot, two Hours will bake it; you may put Sweetmeats in it if you pleaſe.

To make Wigs another Way.

TAKE two Pounds of Flour, and a Qnarter of a Pound of Butter, and as much Sugar; Nutmeg, Cloves and Mace, of each a little; pound in them a Quarter of an Ounce of Carraway ſeeds, a little Barm in as much Cream as will make it in Paſte, mix all together, and work them well; ſet them by the Fire to riſe; when the Oven is ready they will ſoon bake.

To make Bath *Buns.*

TAKE two Pounds of Flour, a Mutchkin of Barm, put a little Brandy in the Barm, and three Eggs well beaten, a little warm Milk, Nutmeg, and a little Salt; rub into the Flour a Pound of Butter, and a Pound of confected Carraways; mix all together, and work it with your

your Hands; ſet them before the Fire to riſe; bake them in a quick Oven, on flour'd Papers, in what Shape you pleaſe.

To make Shrewsbury *Cakes.*

TAKE one Pound of Sugar, three Pounds of Flour, a Nutmeg, and ſome Cinnamon beaten, the Sugar and Spice muſt be ſifted in the Flour; wet it with three Eggs, and as much melted Butter as will make it in a good Thickneſs, to roll into a Paſte; mould it well, and roll it and cut it into what Shape you pleaſe: Prick them before they go into the Oven.

To make Almond Cakes.

TAKE a Pound of Almonds, blanch and beat them very well, with a little Orange-flower Water, beat three Eggs, but two Whites, and put to them a Pound of Sugar ſifted; and then put in your Almonds, and beat all together very well: Butter white Paper, and lay your Cakes in what Form you pleaſe, and bake them.

To make Drop Biſcuit.

TAKE eight Eggs and a Pound of fine Sugar pounded and ſifted, and twelve Ounces of fine Flour well dried; beat your Eggs well, then put in your Sugar and beat it, and then your Flour by Degrees, and beat it all together for an Hour without ceaſing. Your Oven muſt be as hot as for Penny Bread. Then flour ſome Paper, and drop your Biſcuits into what Bigneſs you pleaſe, and put them into the Oven as faſt as you can; and when you ſee them riſe, watch them; and if they begin to colour, take them out again, and put in more; and if the firſt is not enough put them in again: If they are right done they will have a white Ice on them; you may put in Carraway-ſeeds if you pleaſe. When they are all baked, put them into the Oven again, till they are very dry.

To make Marlborough *Cakes*.

TAKE eight Eggs, beat them, and put to them a Pound of Sugar, beaten and sifted, beat it three Quarters of an Hour together; then put in three Quarters of a Pound of fine dry Flour, and two Ounces of Carraway-seeds, beat it all well together, and bake it in a quick Oven in Tin Pans.

A Seed-cake.

TAKE two Pounds of fine Flour well dried, and rub in it a Pound of fresh Butter, and ten Eggs, leaving out five Whites; three Spoonfuls of Cream, four Spoonfuls of good Barm; mix all well together, and set it to the Fire, but not too near; when it is well risen, put in a Pound of confected Carraway. An Hour and a Quarter will bake it.

Another Sort of little Cakes.

TAKE a Pound of Flour, a Pound of Butter, and rub the Butter in the Flour, two Spoonfuls of Barm, and two Eggs: Make it up in a Paste buttered Paper: Roll your Paste out the Thickness of a Crown: Cut them out with the Top of a Tin Canister: Sift fine Sugar over them, and bake them in a slow Oven for an Hour.

To make Whetstone *Cakes.*

TAKE half a Pound of fine Flour, and half a Pound of Loaf-Sugar, pounded and searched, a Spoonful of Carraway Seeds, the Yolk of an Egg, and the Whites of three; a little Rose or Orange-flower Water: Mix all together, and roll it out as thin as a Wafer; cut them with a Glass, lay them on floured Papers, and bake them in a slow Oven.

A Seed-cake very rich.

TAKE a Pound of Flour dried, a Pound of Sugar beaten and sifted, a Pound of Butter work'd with your Hand to a Cream: Beat the Yolks of ten Eggs, six Whites,

Whites, and mix all together; an Ounce of Carraway Seeds, and a Gill of Brandy. Keep it beating till you put it in the Oven.

To make a Plumb-cake.

TAKE four Pounds of fine Flour well dried, five Pounds of Currants well picked and rubbed, five Pounds of Butter beat to a Cream, two Pounds of Almonds beaten fine, thirty four Eggs, half the Whites, two Pounds of fine Sugar beaten and sifted, beaten Mace, Cloves, Ginger, Nutmeg, and two Gills of Brandy: Beat your Sugar first in your Butter, then all the rest by Degrees. You may put in Orange, Lemon-peel candied, and Citron. Keep it beating till you put it in the Oven: Four Hours will bake it.

To ice a great Cake.

TAKE two Pounds of the finest double refined Sugar, and beat and sift it; beat and sift a little Starch, and mix with it; beat six Whites of Eggs to a Froth, and put to it some Gum-water; then mix and beat all this together two Hours, and put it on your Cake; when it is baked, set it in the Oven a Quarter of an Hour.

A rich Nun's Cake.

TAKE four Pounds of fine Flour, and three Pounds of fine Sugar pounded and sifted; dry both by the Fire, beat four Pounds of Butter with your Hands to a Cream; then beat thirty five Eggs, leaving out half the Whites, and beat them and the Butter together, till all appears like Butter. Put in a Gill of Brandy, and beat it again; then take your Flour and Sugar, with six Ounces of Carraway Seeds, and strew it in by Degrees, beating it all the Time for two Hours together. Butter your Hoop, and let it stand three Hours in a moderate Oven.

Sugar Biscuits.

TAKE six Dozen of Eggs, and break them all, keep out one Dozen and a half of the Whites; then take and beat them till they drop like Water; then put in by Degrees half a Stone of Sugar well beat and searched; then beat it till it be extraordinary white and thick. You may know when it is enough, for there will be no red Strings through it; then put in it two Gills of Brandy, and a Quarter of a Pound of Carraway Seeds, then stir in six Fourths of Flour, then drop it upon your Papers, then glaze the Biscuits with fine Sugar before you put them in the Oven. See that the Oven be not too hot.

A Diet Loaf.

TAKE six Eggs, beat them till they drop like Water, and put in twelve Ounces of fine Sugar, well beat and searched; then put in a Spoonful or two of Brandy, and the Grate of two Lemons; mix all together, and beat it with your Whisk well; then put in ten Ounces of Flour, then rub the Frame with Butter, let it stand an Hour in the Oven. Paper the Top, that it may not burn.

To make Saffron Cakes.

TAKE three Pounds of the finest Flour, and dry it before the Fire, mix in it, when it is cold, three Quarters of a Pound of fine powdered Sugar, make a Hole in the Middle of the Flour, beat six Eggs very well and pour them in the Hole, take a Quarter of an Ounce of Saffron, dry and powder it; put it in a Mutchkin of Milk, with half a Pound of Butter, warm it on the Fire; and when the Butter is melted take it off, let it be but just warm: When you pour it to the Flour, whisk among the Eggs three Gills of very good Barm, then put in the Milk and beat it together with your Hands; shake a little Flour on it, and cover it by the Fire till it rises; then mould it in Cakes the Bigness of Bakes: They must have as slow an Oven as

Milk

Milk-bakes, and if they are too stiff, you must put in a little more Milk.

To make Ratafia Biscuits.

POUND and sift a Pound and three Quarters of Loaf Sugar, blanch and beat to a Paste a Pound of bitter Almonds, mix half the Sugar with them, as you are pounding the Almonds keep them wet with Rose-water; beat the Whites of six Eggs to Snow, and mix the rest of the Sugar with them: Then just as you are going to put them in the Oven mix all together; drop them on flour'd Papers, a Spoonful in a Place. The Oven must not be very hot.

To make short Bread.

TAKE a Peck of Flour, make a Hole in the Middle, melt three Pounds of good Butter in a Mutchkin of Barm, put Carraway or what dry Sweet-meats you please in the Flour; then pour in your Butter and Barm, work it well with your Hands, and if too dry, put in a little warm Water; when it is well worked, roll it out in Cakes of what Shape you please. Prick it well with a Fork, and bake it on floured Papers.

To make a Seed Cake.

BEAT sixteen Ounces of good Butter to a Cream, with your Hands; pound and sift sixteen Ounces of Sugar, beat twelve Eggs, the Yolks and Whites separate, a Pound of fine Flour well dried, put in all these by Spoonfuls, keeping the Butter beating all the Time, the Yolks must be beat to Cream, the Whites to a Snow. Don't put in the thin that will fall to the Bottom of the Whites of the Eggs; beat in half an Ounce of Carraway Seeds; when it is beat enough it will come easy off your Hands; put it in your Hoop; two Hours bakes it in not too slow an Oven.

To make Biscuits.

TAKE fifteen Eggs, beat them till they drop like Water off the Whisk; then beat two Pounds of Sugar, and sift it; put in your Sugar by Degrees, and the Grate of an Orange or Lemon, or Carraway Seed, a Pound and an half of Flour, stir all together, drop them by Spoonfuls on floured Paper; don't let the Oven be too hot.

To make white Cakes.

TAKE three Chopins of fine Flour, a Pound and a half of Butter, and a Mutchkin of Cream, two Gills of good Barm, a Gill of Rose-water and Brandy, a little Mace and Nutmegs beaten, nine Eggs, four Whites well beaten, five Ounces of fine Sugar; mix the Sugar and Spice, and a very little Salt with your dry Flour, and keep out a Handful of the Flour, melt the Butter in a little Cream: When a little cold, put the Eggs and Barm in it; make a Hole in the Midst, and pour in all the Flour, stirring it round with your Hand all one Way till well mixed; strew on the Flour you left out, and set it before the Fire to rise, cover'd with a Cloth: Have three Pounds of Currants well wash'd, pick'd and dried; mingle them in the Flour before you wet it; butter your Hoop, set it in a quick Oven, or it will not rise. An Hour and a half bakes it.

To make the thin Dutch *Biscuits.*

TAKE five Pounds of Flour, and two Ounces of Carraway Seed, half a Pound of Sugar, and some more than a Mutchkin of Milk; put into it three Quarters of a Pound of Butter, warm the Milk, and put in a Mutchkin of good Barm; make a Hole in the Middle of your Flour, and pour all in, and make it in a Paste, and let it stand a Quarter of an Hour by the Fire to rise; then mold it, and roll it in Cakes pretty thin; prick them all over pretty much, or they will blister. Bake them a Quarter of an Hour.

To

To mak Quince Cakes.

TAKE two Pounds of dried Flour, beat ſixteen Ounces of ſweet Butter with your Hands till it is in a Cream; then beat twelve Eggs, but half the Whites; pound and ſift fourteen Ounces of fine Sugar, waſh, dry, and pick twelve Ounces of Currants; then mix them all by Degrees, keeping them beating all the Time; put in Nutmeg, Cinnamon and Brandy; when they are beat enough, the Dough will come clean off your Hands; then butter ſome Tart Pans, and bake them not in too hot an Oven, but keep the Oven-door cloſs while they are baking. You may make ſmall Seed-cakes the ſame Way.

York *Cakes.*

TAKE half a Peck of Flour, a Mutchkin of Barm, two Pound of Currants, a Pound of Butter, rub it into the Flour, grate two Nutmegs in it; mix all together with a little Salt and ſome Sugar, wet it with hot Water, it will make twelve Cakes, but let it ly before the Fire to riſe. Bake them in a quick Oven.

To make Naples *Biſcuits.*

TAKE a Pound of fine Sugar pounded and ſifted, a Pound of fine Flour, beat eight Eggs, with two Spoonfuls of Roſe-water; mix the Flour and Sugar, then wet it with the Eggs, and as much cold Water as will make a light Paſte; beat the Paſte very well, then put them in Tin Pans. Bake them in a gentle Oven.

To make Macaroons.

BLANCH and beat a Pound of Almonds very fine, keeping them wetting with Orange-flower Water: Take an equal Quantity of fine Sugar, pounded and ſifted; then beat up the Whites of eight Eggs, and mix them all together; place them handſomely on Wafers, then on Tin Plates or Papers. Bake them in a ſlow Oven.

To make Ginger-bread.

TAKE half a Peck of Flour well dried, five Pounds of Treacle, half a Pound of Butter, two Ounces of beaten Ginger, an Ounce of Carraway Seed; boil the Treacle and Butter together, then mix it with the Flour and Seeds; You may put candied Orange, or Lemon-peel in it: If you please put three Eggs in it, bake them in little Cakes on butter'd Papers.

To make Dutch *Ginger-bread.*

MIX four Pounds of Flour, two Ounces of beaten Ginger; rub in the Flour half a Pound of Butter, and add to it two Ounces of Carraway Seeds, two of Orange-peel dried and rubbed to Powder, two Pounds and a Quarter of Treacle; mix all together, and beat it with a Rolling-pin, and make it up in thirty Cakes; prick them with a Fork, and put them on double buttered Papers.

Poor Knights of Windsor.

TAKE a Roll, and cut it into Slices; soke them in Sack, then dip them in Yolks of Eggs, and fry them; serve them up with beat Butter, Sack and Sugar.

To make Buns.

TAKE two Pounds of Flour, a Mutchkin of Barm; put a little Sack in the Barm, and three Eggs well beat, knead all these together with a little warm Milk, Nutmeg and Salt; then lay it before the Fire till it rises very light, then knead in it sixteen Ounces of sweet Butter, and a Pound of confected Carraway, and bake them in a quick Oven on floured Papers, in what Shape your please.

A Cake to eat hot.

TAKE two Pounds of Flour, rub in it half a Pound of Butter, six Ounces of Sugar, grated Nutmeg and Salt; beat up four Eggs with two Gills of Barm, put as much warm Milk as will make it in a light Dough; work it well, and put it to the Fire to rise: An Hour and

and a half bakes it. You may put half a Pound of Currants, and half a Pound of ston'd Raisins in it, if you please.

A common Breakfast Cake.

TAKE three Quarters of a Pound of Flour, eight Ounces of Butter, four Eggs, half an Ounce of Carraway Seeds; beat it well with your Hands, and bake it in a quick Oven.

Bath *Cakes*.

TAKE a Quart of Flour, a Pound of Butter, ten Ounces of confected Carraways, six Eggs, and but three Whites, six Spoonfuls of Barm, and a little Cream; mix all together, then put them in the Flour, the Butter and Cream must be melted; don't let it be too hot, then put it to the Barm and Eggs; work the Dough well, and set it to the Fire to rise; then shake in the Carraways, and make it into little Cakes, and bake them on floured Papers in a quick Oven.

CHAP. V.

Of PICKLING, *&c.*

RULES to be observed.

ALWAYS use Stone Jars for all Sorts of Pickles that require hot Pickle; for Vinegar and Salt will penetrate through all earthen Vessels: Stone and Glass are the only Things to keep Pickles in: Don't put your Hands in them, but take them up with a Spoon: Let your Brass Pan for any Pickles be very bright and clean, and your Pan for white Pickles well tinned: Use the very best Vinegar, and when they are in the Jars, and cold, melt Sewet, and when it is as cold that it will but just pour on them, put it over them, then cover them with wet Bladders.

To

To pickle Samphire.

IF it is fresh pulled, put it in a Pickle of Salt and Water, that will bear an Egg, changing the Water every four Days, till the Samphire is yellow; then drain it well, and put it in a Brass Kettle, with green Cabbege Leaves over and under them, and as much Water as will cover them, and the Bigness of a Walnut of Roche Allum: Put it on a Fire that will only keep it in a moderate Heat till it is green; then drain it off and dry it with a Cloth; put it in a Jar, and pour on it as much Vinegar boiling hot, with Cloves, Mace, Pepper and sliced Ginger, as will cover it; stop it close; if the Samphire is yellow, and has been in Pickle before, green it the same Way. Observe, that all Sorts of Spices are to be put on Pickles whole, except Nutmeg and Ginger.

To pickle Elder Flowers when they are green, and before they are blown.

LET them ly in a strong Pickle of Salt and Water two Days, then drain them, and put them in a Pan to green, with as much Water as will cover them, and two Gills of Vinegar; put them on a very slow Fire, and put green Blades over and under them; when they are green, dry them with a Cloth, then put them in a Jar, and pour on them as much boiling Vinegar, with Cloves, Mace, Pepper and Ginger in it, as will cover them: Potatoe-apples, and Nasturtian Buds are pickled the same Way.

To pickle Walnuts.

TAKE the Walnuts before the Shells are hard, and make a Pickle of Salt and Water, strong enough to bear an Egg; boil and skim it, and pour it on your Walnuts: Let them ly twenty Days, changing the Pickle every five Days, and boiling it every Time; then take them out, and wipe them with a Cloth: Boil as much white Wine Vinegar as will cover them, with Pepper, Cloves, Mace, Ginger and Nutmeg quartered; slice

ſlice the Ginger, and let all the reſt be whole: To a hundred of Walnuts, put ſix Spoonfuls of Muſtard-ſeed, and ſix Cloves of Garlick: When your Walnuts, Muſtard, and Garlick are in the Jar, pour your Vinegar and Spice boiling hot on them; prick them full of Holes before you put them in the Salt and Water.

To pickle Walnuts green.

TAKE the largeſt and cleareſt you can get before the Shells are hard; pare them very thin, and as you pare them, throw them in Spring-water; put into the Water a Pound of Bay-ſalt; let them ly in it Twenty-four Hours; take them out and put them in a Jar, and between every Lair of Walnuts lay a Lair of Vine-leaves, and alſo at the Top and Bottom; then fill it up with cold Vinegar; let them ſtand all Night, then pour the Vinegar from them into a Bell-metal Sauce-pan, with a Pound of Bay-ſalt, and let it boil; pour it hot on your Nuts, cover them cloſs, and let them ſtand a Week; pour off that Pickle, and rub them with a Piece of Flannel; then put them in the Jar with Vine-leaves, as before, and boil freſh Vinegar with Cloves, Mace, Ginger, Nutmeg, and Pepper; pour it boiling hot on them every Day for four Days, then put in with them a little Muſtard-ſeed, and either Garlick or Shalots.

To pickle Muſhrooms.

TAKE the ſmall hard white Buttons, put them in Water, and wipe them with a Bit of clean white Flannel till all the Spots or black is off them, and as you wipe them throw them in clean Water; then put them in a Pan of clean cold Water, with the Bigneſs of a Nut of Allum, and put them on the Fire; don't let them boil, but coming to it; take them off, and ſpread them on a Cloth, and cover them with another; have ready boiled as much white Wine Vinegar as will cover them, white Pepper, Cloves, Mace, Ginger in it; they muſt be all whole: Don't put on the Vinegar till cold;

put

put a little ſweet Oil on the Top of the Bottle you put them in. Obſerve, that all the Water you put them in muſt be cold.

To pickle Onions.

TAKE ſmall Onions, put them in a Pan of cold Water on the Fire, and when they are coming to boil, take them off, and take off all the brown Skins; lay them between two Cloths till cold, then put them in Bottles, and boil white Wine Vinegar, Pepper, Mace, Cloves, Ginger, and pour it on them.

To pickle red Cabbage.

CUT the Cabbage in thin Shaves; put it in a Goblet with a Gill of Vinegar, and a little Salt; put it on the Fire cloſs covered, and let it ly for ten Minutes, ſhaking the Goblet very often; then put it in a well glazed Can, and boil as much Vinegar as will cover it, with whole Pepper, Cloves, Mace, and ſliced Ginger; pour it on boiling hot; cover it cloſs. It will be fit for eating in four Days.

To pickle Cucumbers, or Kidney-beans.

PUT them in a ſtrong Pickle of Salt and Water for four Days; then drain them off, and dry them in a Cloth; put them in a Braſs Pan with green Cabbage-leaves under and over them, with as much Water as will cover them, and a little Bit of Roche Allum; put them on a very ſlow Fire, and change the Blades when they turn yellow; when they are very hot, take off the Pan till they are cold, then put it on again; put it on and off till they are green, then put them in a Cloth and dry them; boil white Wine Vinegar, whole Pepper, *Jamaica* Pepper, Cloves, and ſliced Ginger, and when they are in the Jar, pour it on them boiling hot; cover them cloſs. You may pickle any green Pickles the ſame Way.

To

To pickle Cucumbers in Slices.

CUT large green Cucumbers in Slices, not too thin, put them in a broad Pan with ſome ſmall peeled Onions; let them ſtand twenty-four Hours cloſe cover'd; then put them in a Sieve to drain: Boil as much Vinegar as will cover them, whole Pepper, Mace, Ginger, and a little Salt; and when they are in the Jar pour it boiling hot on them: Cover them cloſe, boil the Vinegar every Day for four or five Days, then they will be fit for Uſe.

To pickle Mangoes.

TAKE the largeſt green Cucumbers you can get, and cut a Piece out of the Side, and take out all the Seeds; fill them with Muſtard, whole Pepper, Cloves, Mace, and Ginger ſliced; put in them Garlick, or Rockambole or Shalots; then put in the Piece you cut out of the Side, and tye it faſt: Green them as you do Cucumbers; dry them, put them in a Jar, pour over them Vinegar boiling hot. Let all Sorts of Spice be boil'd in it.

To pickle Colliflowers.

TAKE Colliflowers, when then they are as big as an Egg, cloſs and white, and juſt give them a Scald in boiling Water, then ſpread them on a Cloth, and cover them with it, boil the beſt Vinegar with whole white Pepper, Mace and Cloves; and when they are dry put them in a Jar, and pour the Vinegar when cold on them. You may pickle white Cabbage Stalks and young Turneps the ſame Way, but pare the Turneps, and cut them the Bigneſs of Muſhrooms.

To pickle Colliflowers red.

CUT them in ſmall Pieces, but leave on them a ſhort Stalk, put in a Chopin of Vinegar, three Pennyworth of Cocheneal, a little *Jamaica* and black Pepper, and a little Salt, boil it, and pour it hot over the Colliflowers: Let it ſtand two or three Days cloſs covered;

ſcald it every three Days till it is red. The Cocheneal muſt be very finely pounded.

To pickle Aſparagus.

TAKE the largeſt Aſparagus that is very green, cut off the White, and ſcrape them lightly to the Head, then put them in a Jar, and throw over them ſome Salt, and a few Cloves and Mace, and pour on them as much Vinegar as will cover them: Let them lye nine Days, then put the Vinegar in a Braſs Kettle, and put the Aſparagus into it, ſtow them down cloſs; let them ſtand a little, then ſet them on the Fire until they are green; then put them in a Jar, and tye them cloſe.

To pickle Plumbs like Olives.

MAKE a Pickle of Water, Vinegar, white Wine and Fennel-ſeed; boil it; put in as much of each as will give the Pickle a Taſte; then put in the Plumbs, and take them off the Fire preſently. Let them ſtand till they are cold, and put them in Bottles.

To pickle Sellery.

CUT Sellery two Inches long, put them in *Salt* and Water when it boils, and let them boil two or three Minutes; let them cool, and boil Vinegar, Pepper, Cloves and Ginger; and when cold pour it on them.

To pickle Codlins like Mangoes.

GET Codlins full grown, but not full ripe, put them in Salt and Water that will bear an Egg, let them lye in it nine Days, ſhift the Pickles every two Days, then dry them; take out the Stalk ſo whole that it may fit again; and ſcoop out the Core, but leave the Eye in them; fill in the Room of the Core, with whole Muſtard, a Clove of Garlick, Pepper, Mace and Cloves: Put in your Piece and tye it up tight, boil as much Vinegar as will cover them, whole Pepper, Cloves, Mace,

and

and sliced Ginger; pour it boiling hot upon them every Day for a Fortnight. Cover them close.

To make Gooseberry Vinegar.

BRUISE the Gooseberries with your Hand when they are full ripe, and to every Chopin of Gooseberries put three Chopins of Water boil'd, and let it be put cold on them, and let it stand twenty-four Hours, then strain it through Canvas, or Flannel; to four Chopins of it put a Pound of brown Sugar, stir it well and put it in a Barrel; let it lye three Quarters of a Year, but the longer the better: It is good for Pickling.

Mushroom Powder.

TAKE a Fourth-part of large Mushrooms, rub them clean, but don't take out the Inside or Skins; put to them sixteen Blades of Mace, forty Cloves, a Spoonful of Pepper, and a Handful of Salt, the Bigness of an Egg of Butter, two Gills of Vinegar; let all stew fast on the Fire, keep them stirring till they have spent their Liquor, keep the Liquor for any savoury Dishes, and dry the Mushrooms first on a Dish in the Oven, then on Sieves, till they are dry enough to pound. It will keep four or five Years, and a little of it will relish any Meat Dish.

To codle the right Codlin with Cream.

PUT the Codlins in a Stew-pan, with as much Water as will cover them; set them on a slow Fire till the Skin peels off them, then take them up and peel them; put them in a very thin Syrup, with some of the Leaves of Apple Trees: Cover them closs, and put them on the Fire again, and let them simmer, but not boil: When they are green and tender, clarify half a Pound of Sugar, and boil the Codlins in it: Set them to simmer on a very slow Fire, then set them to cool, and boil half a Mutchkin of Cream; thicken it with the Yolks of three Eggs: Put in it two Spoonfuls of Rose-water, sweeten

ſweeten it to your Taſte, and when it is cold, pour it over the Apples.

To keep Fruit for Tarts.

PULL the Gooſe-berries before they are full ripe, pick off the black Eyes and the Stems; get wide mouthed Bottles, that are very dry and ſweet, put your Gooſe-berries in them, cork the Bottles well, put them in an Oven almoſt cold, and let them ly in it till they turn white; then take out the Bottles, and when they are cold, roſin the Corks, and put them in a cold, but not a damp Place. You may bottle red, white and black Currants, but they muſt be ripe.

To keep Damſons or ſmall Plumbs for Tarts.

PUT them in a Lime Can: To ſix Pounds of Damſons put three Pounds of *Lisbon* Sugar, then put coarſe Paſte on the Can, and put it in the Oven for an Hour; when you are going to make Uſe of them, take them up with a Horn or Wooden Spoon: Never put your Hand in any preſerved Fruit, for it will ſpoil them.

To make a Pupton of Apples.

PARE ſome Apples, take out the Cores, put them in a Sauce-pan, and chop them groſly; to three Mutchkins of theſe Apples put in a Quarter of a Pound of Sugar, and two Spoonfuls of Water: Put them on a ſlow Fire, keep them ſtirring, grate the Rind of an Orange and Lemon in it: When it is quite thick as Marmalade, let it ſtand till cold; then beat up the Yolks of four Eggs, and ſtir in a Handful of grated Bread, and a Quarter of a Pound of ſweet Butter: Mix them all together, form it into what Shape you pleaſe, and bake it in a ſlow Oven; then put it on a Plate upſide down, for a ſecond Courſe or Supper.

To

To make black Caps.

CUT twelve large Apples in Halves, and take out the Cores; place them on a white Iron Patty-pan with their Skins on; put to them four Spoonfuls of Rose-water, and grate fine Sugar over them; set them in a hot Oven till the Skins are black a little, and the Apples tender, so serve them up; and when you dish them, grate more Sugar over them.

To bake Apples.

PUT your Apples in an Earthen Can, with a few Cloves, a little Lemon-peel, coarse Sugar, and a Glass of red Wine; cover them close; they will take an Hour's Baking in a quick Oven. You may do Pears the same Way, but they will take two Hours Baking.

To stew Apples in Halves.

PARE them, and cut them in Halves, and take out the Cores: To eight Apples, put a Chopin of Water, a Quarter of a Pound of Sugar, the Rind of a Lemon and Orange cut in small Strings; put them in a Pan, cover them, and put them over the Fire; when they are soft, serve them up with Lemon and Orange-peel about them, and the Syrup. You may do them the same Way, without taking off the Skin.

To preserve Apples for Tarts, or Torts, for a Year.

PULL the right Sort of white Codlins, when they are no bigger than large Walnuts, and some of the Leaves; put them in a Pan of cold Water, and put them on a slow Fire; when they turn white, take them up one by one, lay them on a Cloth, don't let them touch one another; cover them till both them and their Liquor is cold, then put them in a well glaz'd Can, and pour the Liquor over them; pour some render'd Sewet over them, and tye them up close with a Bladder: When you are going to use them, take off their Skin, and put them, a little of their own Liquor,

Liquor, and a Bit of fine Loaf-sugar in a preserving Pan; cover them with Water, put green Kail-leaves over them, and set them on a slow Fire till they are green, then boil up a Syrup of fine Sugar, and put them in it, and let them simmer in it for an Hour. You may send them when cold to Table, in the Syrup with Rose-water in it, or bake them in Tarts, or Torts.

To make a Caudle for Apple or Goose-berry Torts.

BOIL a half Mutchkin of Cream, with a Stick of Cinnamon, the Rind of a Lemon, and a little Sugar; thicken it with the Yolks of two Eggs: When your Tort is cold, and your Cream, put in it two or three Spoonfuls of Rose-water, and pour it over the Tort.

To preserve Goose-berries green.

TAKE the fairest green Goose-berries and largest, pick off the black Tops, and caudle them in fair Water; then peel them, and put them into the warm Water as you peel them: When they are all done, set them over a very slow Fire not to boil, and cover them closs till they look very clear and green; have ready some Jelly of Goose-berries made of the greenest Gaskins, boil it uncovered very fast till they are to Pieces; strain out the Jelly and the Goose-berries into it, and the same Weight of fine Sugar; boil and skim them till they are enough, then glass them up.

To preserve Pears.

TAKE the best preserving Pears fresh pulled, make a small Hole at the black End, and pick out the Seeds with a Needle-head; then put them in scalding Water, and take the Skin off them; then take their equal Weight of fine Sugar, and take the same Water your Pears were boiled in, and mix the Sugar with as much of the Water as will cover the Pears; then let it come a-boiling, and skim it; put in your Pears, and let them boil till they be soft, then take them out, and boil up your

your Syrup; and when they are both cold, lay in your Pears in Gallypots; pour the Syrup over them before you boil them, put a Clove in every Hole, pour Jelly of Apples over them, and they will keep a great while.

To preserve Raspberries whole.

TAKE the fairest and largest Rasp-berries you can get, and to every Pound of Rasps, add a Pound and a half of fine Sugar; clarify it and boil it till it blows very strong, put in the Rasps, and let them boil as quick as possible, strewing some fine beat Sugar on them as they boil: When the Sugar boils over them, take them off, and let them stand to cool, then put them on the Fire again; put to every Pound of Rasps two Gills of Currant Jelly; then boil it till the Syrup hangs in Flax from the Spoon, keep them well skimmed, then put them in Glasses when they are almost cold.

To make Raspberry Jam.

PICK them clean, and to every Pound of Rasps put two Gills of Currant Juice, and a Pound and a half of Sugar; boil them on a quick Fire, and when they fall to the Bottom, they are enough.

To preserve the green admirable Plumb.

TAKE these Plumbs when full grown, and just on the Turn; prick them with a large Needle, and set them on the Fire with as much Water as will cover them, with green Kail-leaves under and over them; let them green very gradually, they must not boil; then drain them, and boil them in clarified Sugar, let them cool a little, and give them another Boil if they shrink; prick them with a Fork in the Syrup, and give them another Boil; put a Sheet of clean white Paper over them, and set them by; next Day boil some Sugar till it blows, and put it to them, and give them a good Boil, then put them by for Use.

To preserve Goose-berries whole.

TAKE the largest preserving Goose-berries, and pick off the black Eye, but not the Stalk; set them over the Fire in a Pot of Water to scald; cover them very closs, and let them scald, but not boil, or break, and when they are tender, take them up in cold Water; then take a Pound and a Half of double refined Sugar to a Pound of Goose-berries; clarify the Sugar with Water, and when the Syrup is cold, put your Goose-berries into your preserving Pan, and put the Syrup to them; set them on a gentle Fire, and let them boil, but not too fast, lest they break; when you perceive the Sugar has entered them, take them off; cover them with white Pepper, and set them by till the next Day, then take them out of the Syrup, and boil the Syrup till it begins to rope; skim it and put it to them again, and set them on a gentle Fire till you perceive the Syrup will rope; then take them off, and when cold cover them with Paper; boil some Goose-berries to Jelly, and put them in Glasses, and cover them with it.

To scald Fruit for present Use.

PUT your Fruit in boiling Water, as much as will cover them; set them on a slow Fire till they are tender, turning them often; lay a Paper closs on them; let them stand till cold. To a Pound of Fruit put half a Pound of Sugar; let it boil, but not fast, till it looks clear: If you do whole Pipins, you must cut Orange and Lemon-peel as small as Straw, and put them and the Juice of Lemon in them.

To make white Quince Marmalade.

SCALD your Quinces tender, take off the Skin, and pulp them from the Core very fine: To every Pound of Quinces put a Pound and a half of fine Sugar in Lumps, and two Gills of Water; dip your Sugar in Water, and boil and skim it till it is a thick Syrup;

Syrup, then put in your Quinces. Boil it on a quick Fire.

To preserve Apricocks.

PULL the fairest Apricocks before they are too ripe, wipe them, and put them in a Pan of cold Water; set them on the Fire, and when the Water is just scalding hot, take them off and skin them, and as you skin them, grate Sugar on them: If there are any Bits that want Skin pare it off very thin with a Pen-knife; then take out the Stones on the Side that has a Cress in it, but don't break the Apricock: If there are any very hard to come out, let them alone till they are boiled in the Syrup. To every Pound of them put a Pound of very fine Loaf-sugar; dip it in Water, and boil it; skim it, and then put in the Apricocks; let them ly in it till the Syrup is cold, then put them on a slow Fire, and let them simmer, cover them with a clean Sheet of Paper; take them off again, and let them cool; break the Stones, and take out your Kernels whole, put them in with the Apricocks; put them on and off the Fire three or four times, still letting them cool till the Syrup penetrates into them, then let them boil till they are clear, take care they don't break; never let them boil till the last Time, only simmer; then put them in Gallypots, and when cold, paper them. Take the Skins off the Kernels.

To preserve red or white Currants whole.

PULL the largest Branches and biggest Kernels you can get; make a very small Slit in the Side of them with a Needle, and pick out the Seeds; hold them very gently in your Fingers, for Fear of bruising or pulling them off the Stems: To every Pound of Currants, you must have two Pounds of clarified double refined Sugar, and put the Currants in it on a clear Fire: The red must have half a Mutchkin of the Juice of red Currants in it, and you must boil both till they are quite clear on a quick Fire.

To preserve Pears red.

TAKE the large Pound Pears, when full ripe, pare them, and put them in as much Water as will cover them, then put in a Penny-worth of pounded Cocheneal, and let them boil till they are tender; then put in the Weight of your Pears of Sugar, and let it boil to a thick Syrup; cover your Pears till you boil and skim your Syrup; then put in your Pears, and let them boil till they are red and clear: put the Rind of a Lemon and Orange cut in Strings, and squeeze in the Juice in the Syrup before it comes to boil: Put them in Gallypots, and put on them the Jelly of red Goose-berries, it is made as the Jelly of green Goose-berries.

To make Marmalade of Oranges.

TAKE your Oranges, grate them, cut them in Quarters, take the Skins off them, and take the Pulp from the Strings and Seeds; put the Skins in a Pan of Spring-water, boil them till they are very tender, then take them out of the Water, and cut them in very thin Slices; beat some in a Marble Mortar, and leave the thin Slices to boil by themselves. To every Pound of Oranges put a Pound of fine Sugar; first wet the Sugar in Water, boil it a good while, then put in Half of the Pulp, keep the other Half for the sliced Oranges; to every Mutchkin of the Pulp you must put in a Pound of Sugar likeways, then put in the grated Rind, boil it till it is very clear, then put it in Gallypots; when cold, paper them. Boil your Chips the same Way, but don't mix the pounded with them.

To preserve Goose-berries for Tarts.

PICK them clean, and to every ten Pounds of Goose-berries put eight Pounds of fine powdered Sugar, and two Gills of Water; put them on a slow Fire till the Sugar is well simmered among them; skim them, and then let them boil as fast as you please: Boil them till they are very clear and will jelly. You may preserve green

green Gaskens, and red and white Goosberries for Tarts, the same Way.

To preserve white Plumbs.

TAKE your Plumbs before they are too ripe, give them a Slit in the Seam, and prick them behind, make your Water almost scalding hot, and put a little Sugar into it, and put in your Plumbs, and cover them close, set them on the Fire to coddle, and take them off a little and set them on again; take care they do not break; boil to a Height as much refined Sugar as will cover them; and when they are coddled pretty tender, take them out of the Liquor, and put them into your preserving Pan to your Syrup, which must be Blood-warm: Let them boil till they are clear, skim them, and take them off, and let them stand two Hours, then set them on, and boil them again; when they are clear put them in Glasses, boil your Syrup till it is thick, and when cold pour it on your Plumbs. Put Jelly of Pipins over them.

To preserve Damsons.

TAKE some Damsons, and cut them in Pieces, and put them in in a Skellet over the Fire, with as much Water as will cover them; when they boil, and the Liquor pretty strong, strain it out: Add for every Pound of your whole Damsons a Pound of double refined Sugar, put the third Part of the Sugar in the Liquor, and set it on the Fire, and when it simmers put in your whole Damsons, wipe them clean, let them have one good Boil, take them off for half an Hour, and cover them up close; then set them on again, and let them simmer over the Fire, often turning them: Take them out, and put them in a Bason, and strew all the Sugar you left on them, and pour the hot Liquor over them, and cover them up, and let them stand till next Day; then boil them up again till they are enough, take them up and put them in Pots; boil the Liquor

Liquor till it jellies, and pour it on them when it is almost cold, so paper them.

To preserve green Plumbs.

TAKE green Plumbs before they begin to ripen, let them be carefully gathered, with their Stalks and Leaves, put them in cold Spring-water over a Fire, and let them boil very gently; when they will peel take off the Skins, and put the Plumbs in other cold Water; and let them stand over a very gentle Fire till they are soft; put two Pounds of double refined Sugar to every Pound of Plumbs, and make the Sugar with some Water into a very thick Syrup. Before the Plumbs are put in it, the Stones of the Plumbs must be as soft as you may thrust a Pin in them. After the same Manner do green Apricocks.

To preserve Mulberries.

SET some Mulberries on the Fire, and draw from them a Mutchkin of Juice, put to it three Pounds of Sugar; boil your Syrup and skim it, and put into it two Pounds of ripe Mulberries, and let them stand in the Syrup till they are thoroughly warm, then set them on the Fire, and let them boil gently, then put them by till next Day, then boil them; and when the Syrup is pretty thick, and the Drop stands, they are enough; so put them in Glasses, and paper them when cold.

Jelly of Goose-berries.

TAKE your Goose-berries when they are at full Growth, but not ripe; fill a Pint-stoup, and stop the Mouth of it, and put it in a Pot of Water, and let it boil till they are tender; then put them in a Search, and let the Juice drain from them; then fill up the Stoup again, and do so till you have stewed all you have a-mind to do; to every Mutchkin of Juice put a Pound and a Quarter of fine Sugar, and when dissolved, boil it as you did the Apple-Jelly.

To

To preserve golden Pipins red.

PARE them, and make a Hole in them through the Heart with a Skewer; put them in a Pan with as much Water as will cover them; put a Penny-worth of Cocheneal in a Bit of Musling, and put it in; cut the Rind of a Lemon and Orange in long small Strings, and put that and the Juice in them; let them simmer till they are a little tender, then put in two Pounds of fine Loaf-sugar to a Dozen, and let it dissolve; then put them on a quick Fire, and let them boil very fast till they are a clear red, and very tender; the faster they boil, the wholler they will be. You must not cover them at all, but stand and keep them under the Syrup with a Silver-spoon, they take a long Time to boil. You may do them clear the same Way, leaving out the Cocheneal. A Bath-metal Skellet is the best to do them in.

To make Marmalade of Plumbs, or any Fruit.

PUT them in a Stoup, and put the Stoup in a Pot of Water; let it stew till they are very tender, then rub them through a Search; put to them their equal Weight of fine Sugar, and boil them to a Marmalade; break the Sugar very small before you put it in the Marmalade.

To make a Syrup of Nettles.

PICK the young red Nettles in *April*, and put them in a Pint-stoup; put the Stoup in a Pot of Water, and let them simmer for twelve Hours, then squeeze out the Tincture, and put it in a clean Pan, beat the Whites of two Eggs and mix with it; and when it boils, skim it, and to every Mutchkin of Tincture put a Pound of brown Sugar-candy: When it is dissolved, set it on the Fire and boil it up to a Syrup, then let it cool, and bottle it, put no Water to the Nettles. —— They are good for Consumptions.

Syrup

Syrup of Maiden-hair.

FILL a Pint-stoup as much as it will hold, and put as much Water as will cover it, and set it on the Side of the Fire, and let it stand twenty four Hours, then try if all the Taste be from it, if not, set it nearer the Fire, and let it boil, then strain it, and to every Mutchkin of the Tincture put a Pound of white Sugar-candy, and two Drops of Cinnamon, and a Drop of Mace, they must be whole, boil all together to a Syrup, and when cold, bottle it. You may make any Herb-syrup the same Way.

To make Jelly of Apples the Colour of Amber.

TAKE big Pipins, pare them, and take out the Cores, and boil them in a Chopin of Water till it comes to a Mutchkin; put in it two Spoonfuls of Rose-water, a Pound of fine Sugar, boil it uncovered till it comes to the right Colour; drop a little on a Piece of Glass, and if it stands upright, it is enough; put it in Glasses or Gally-pots. You may make red Jelly the same Way, but colour the Water with a little Cocheneal.

Goose-berry Jam.

TAKE the green Goose-berries full ripe, top and tail them, and weigh them; put a Pound of Fruit to three Quarters of a Pound of fine Sugar, and two Gills of Water; boil the Sugar and Water together, skim it, and put in your Goose-berries, and boil them till they are clear and tender, then put them in Pots.

To preserve Cherries.

TAKE the best Morello Cherries when full ripe, either stone them, or clip off Part of the Stalks; to every Pound take a Pound of Sugar, and boil it till it blows very strong; then put in your Cherries, and by Degrees bring them to boil as fast as you can, that the Sugar may come over them; skim them, and set them by, next Day boil a Mutchkin of the Juice of red

red Currants, and a Pound of Sugar, and skim it, and put it in the Cherries, then give all a Boil together: When almost cold, place them in Glasses, and pour the Syrup on them.

To make Currant Jelly.

MASH the Currants, and put them on the Fire, then squeeze out all the Juice, and to every *English* Quart, put two Pounds of Sugar; put it on the Fire and boil it, keep it well skimmed, and stir it till the Sugar dissolves: When it boils twelve Minutes, drop a little on a Plate, and if it jellies, take it off and put it in Glasses, the finer the Sugar is, the better for all Sweet-meats: If it is white Currants, clarify the Sugar, and strain the Juice.

To make Conserve of Roses.

TAKE the Scarlet Buds before they are ripe, and cut off all the Whites, then weigh all the Roses, and put them into a Mortar, and beat them extraordinary well, till they be like Powder; then take the triple Weight of your Roses in Sugar, well searched, and put it in by Degrees, always beating them; and as it dissolves, put in more, till your Sugar be all made Use of; and when it is all well mixed, put it up in your Gallypots, and set it against the Sun; stir them once in two or three Days for a Fortnight, then it is fit for Use: After this Manner you may make Conserve of Violets or Gilliflowers.

Clear Pipin Jelly.

TAKE fourteen good Pipins, and throw them into cold Water; set them on the Fire till they are dissolved, then strain them, and to a Mutchkin of it put a Pound of double refined Sugar; let it boil very fast, and keep it clean skimmed; then put in it the Juice of two large Lemons: As it is boiling, try it on a Plate, and

and when you find it jellies, it is enough. You may put a Chopin of Water in it.

Jelly of Pipins with Slices.

BOIL a Mutchkin of Water, and a Pound of Sugar, with six Pipins, the Juice of a Lemon and Orange, to a clear Jelly; then pare and core three Pipins, and cut them in Slices, and put them in your Jelly, and boil them very quick, till they are clear, but don't let them break, so put them in Glasses.

To colour Jellies.

JELLIES made of Hartshorn or Calves Feet, may be made of what Colour you please. If white, use Almonds pounded and strained after the usual Manner; if yellow, put in Yolks of Eggs, or a little *Saffron* steeped and squeezed; if red, some Juice of Beet-root or Cocheneal; if Purple, Turnsole or Powder of Violets; if green, Juice of Beets or Spinage.

A very fine Way to dry Cherries.

TO every five Pound of ston'd Cherries, take a Pound of double refined Sugar; put the Cherries into the preserving Pan, with a very little Water: Make both but just scalding hot, take them immediately out of this Liquor, and dry them; then put them again into the Pan, and strew on Sugar between every Lair of Cherries; let it stand to melt, and then set it on the Fire, and make it scalding hot, as before; which must be done twice or thrice with the Sugar; then drain them from the Syrup, and lay them singly to dry in the Sun, or in the Stove. When they are dry, throw them into a Bason of cold Water, and take them immediately out, and dry them with a Cloth; set them again in the hot Sun, or in the Stove; and keep them in a dry Place all the Year. This is not

not only the best Way to give them a good Taste, but also the most certain Way for Colour and Plumpness.

Currants preserved in Bunches.

STONE your Currants, and tye them up in small Bunches: To every Pound of Currants, boil two Pounds of Sugar, till it blows very strong; then slip in the Currants, and give them a quick Boil, till the Sugar covers them; let them settle a Quarter of an Hour, then let them boil till the Sugar rises almost to the Top of the Pan; then let them settle, skim them, and set them by till next Day, then drain them, and lay them out, taking Care to spread out the Sprigs, that they may not stick together; then dust them well, and dry them in a hot Stove.

Currants in Jelly.

STRIP the Currants, and put them in an Earthen Pot, tye them close down, and set them in a Kettle of boiling Water, and let them stand three Hours, the Kettle still boiling; then take a clean flaxen Cloth, and strain out the Juice; and when it is settled, take a Pound of double refined Sugar beaten and sifted, and put to it a Mutchkin of clear Juice: Have ready some whole Currants ston'd, and put them in when the Juice boils, and let them boil till the Syrup jellies, which you may know by trying it in a Spoon, then put it in Glasses. Make Jelly of Currants the same Way, only leave out the whole Currants. When cold, paper them up.

To preserve Rasp-berries liquid.

TAKE the fairest and largest Rasp-berries you can get, and to every Pound of Rasps, take a Pound and a half of Sugar, clarify it, and boil it till it blows very strong: Put in the Rasps, and let them boil as quick as possible, strewing some fine beat Sugar on them as they boil: When they have had a good Boil, and that the Sugar rises all over them, take them off, and let them settle a little; then give them another Boil, and put to every Pound of Rasps half a Pint of Currant Jelly; give them a good Boil, till you perceive the Syrup hangs in Flaiks from your Skimmer, then take them from the Fire, take off the Scum, and put them into Glasses or Pots. Take the Scum clean off the Top; when cold, make a Jelly of Currants, and fill up your Glasses; cover them with Paper, first wet in Water, and dried a little betwixt two Cloths, which Paper you must put close to the Jelly, then wipe the Glasses clean, and cover the Tops with the dry Paper.

Raspberry Cakes.

PICK away all the Stems and spotted Raspberries, then bruise the rest through a Hair-sieve into an earthen Pan, and put on a Board or Weight to press out all the Water you can; then pour the Paste into the Preserving-pan, and dry it over the Fire till there is no Moisture in it, that is, no Juice that will run from it, stirring it closs to keep it from burning: To every Pound take a Pound and two Ounces of Sugar finely beat, and put it in gradually: When all is in put it on the Fire, and let it incorporate well together; then take it off and scrape it all to one Side of the Pan, let it cool a very little, and put it into Moulds; when quite cold, put them into the Stove without dusting, and dry it as other Paste. Take care the Paste does not boil after the Sugar is in, for it will make it greasy, and hinder it to dry.

Raspberry clear Cakes.

TAKE two Quarts of ripe Goose-berries, and a Quart of red Raspberries; put them into a Stone Jug, and stop them closs; then set them into a Pot of cold Water, as much as covers the Neck of the Jug, and let it boil till it comes to a Paste; then put them into a Hair-sieve, and press out all the Jelly into a Pan, and strain it through a Jelly-bag. To every Pound put

put twenty Ounces of double refined Sugar, and boil it till it crack in the Water; then take it off, and put in the Jelly, and ſtir it over a ſlow Fire till all the Sugar is melted; then give it a good Fleet till it is well incorporated; then take it off and ſkim it well, and fill your clear Cake Glaſſes; take off the Skim, and put it into the Stove to dry. When they begin to cruſt on the upper Side, turn them out upon ſquare Glaſſes, and ſet them to dry again. When they begin to have a tender Candy, cut them into Quarters, or as you pleaſe, and ſet them to dry till hard; then turn them on Sieves, and when thoroughly dry, put them into Boxes. In filling up your clear Cakes and clear Paſte, you muſt be as expeditious as poſſible; for if it cools, it will be a Jelly before you can get it in. White Raſpberry clear Cakes are made the ſame Way, only mixing them with the Gooſe-berries in the Infuſion.

To preſerve green Amber Plumbs.

TAKE green Amber Plumbs when full grown, prick them in two or three Places, and put them in cold Water; ſet them over the Fire to ſcald, and take care not to let the Water become too hot, leſt it ſpoil them: When they are very tender, put them into a very thin Sugar, that is to ſay, one Part Sugar and two Parts Water; give them a little Warm in it, and ſet them by covered: Next Day give them another Warm, and the third Day drain them, and boil up the Syrup, adding a little more Sugar; then put the Syrup to the Plumbs, and give them a Warm. Next Day do the ſame; the Day following boil the Syrup till it is a little ſmooth, put in the Plumbs, and give them a Boil; the next Day boil the Syrup till very ſmooth, put it to the Plumbs and cover them, and put them in the Stove; next Day boil ſome Sugar to blow very ſtrong; put it to the Fruit, and give all a Boil, then put it into the Stove for two Days; then drain them, and lay them

on

out to dry; first dusting them very well, and manage them in the drying as any other Fruit.

To preserve the green Mogul Plumb.

LET it be just upon the turning ripe, prick it into the Stone on that Side where the Clift is with a Penknife, and as you do them throw them into cold Water, and set them over a very slow Fire to scald; when they are very tender take them carefully out of the Water, and put them into a thin Sugar, half Sugar, half Water; warm them gently, cover them and set them by: The next Day drain off the Syrup and boil it smooth, adding a little fresh Sugar, and give them a gentle Boil; the Day following boil the Sugar very smooth, and pour it on them, and set them in the Stove for two Days; then drain them, and boil fresh Sugar very smooth, just to blow a little; put in your Plumbs, and give them a good covered Boiling; skim them and put them into the Stove for two Days; drain them and lay them out to dry, dusting them very well.

To preserve yellow Amber Plumbs.

TAKE them when full ripe, put them into the preserving Pan with as much Sugar as will cover them, and give them a good Boil; let them settle a litttle, and give them another Boil three or four times round the Fire, skim them, and next Day drain off the Syrup; put them again into the Pan, and boil as much fresh Sugar as will cover them to blow. Give them a thorough Boiling, and skim them, and set them in the Stove Twenty-four Hours; then drain them, and lay them out to dry. Dust them first.

To preserve green Grapes.

TAKE the largest and finest Grapes before they are thorough ripe, stone them and scald them, and let them ly two Days in the Water they are scalded in; then

then drain them and put them into a thin Syrup, and give them a Heat over a slow Fire: Next Day turn them in the Pan, and warm them again: Next Day drain them, and give them a good Boil in clarified Sugar, and skim them and set them by: The Day following boil some Sugar to blow, and put in the Grapes, and give them a good Boil; skim them, and set them in a warm Stove all Night; drain them next Day, and lay them out to dry, having dusted them well.

Green Apricocks.

TAKE them before the Stones are hard, wet them and lay them in a coarse Cloth with two or three Handfuls of Salt, and rub them till the Roughness is off; then put them in scalding Water, and let them be almost boiled; then set them off till almost cold, do this two or three Times: After this let them be close covered, and when they look green, let them boil till they begin to be tender; take their Weight of double refined Sugar, and to a Pound of Sugar two Gills of Water; make the Syrup, and when it is almost cold, put in the Apricocks, boil them till they are clear; warm your Syrup three or four Times till it is thick. You may put them in cold Jelly, or dry them as you use them.

Apricock Chips.

SLICE the Apricocks the long Way, but not pare them; take their Weight of double refined Sugar, boil it to a thin Candy, put in the Apricocks and let them stand on the Fire till they are scalding hot; let them ly a Night in the Liquor, then lay them on thin Plates, and set them in the Sun to dry.

Jam Apricocks.

PARE them and take out the Stones, break them and take out the Kernels, and blanch them; to every Pound of Apricocks boil a Pound of Sugar till it blows very strong, put in the Apricocks and give them a quick

quick Boil till they are broke, then take them off and bruise them well; put in the Kernels and stir all together on the Fire, and fill your Pots or Glasses with them. If it is too sweet, sharpen it with a little white Currant Jelly to your Taste.

To preserve green Walnuts.

GATHER them in fair Weather, and before the Shell grows hard; boil them in Water to take off the Bitterness, then put them into cold Water; peel off the Rind, and lay them in a Pan with a Lair of Sugar equal to the Weight of the Nuts, and as much Water as will wet it. When they are boiled up over a moderate Fire and cooled, do the same Thing again, and set them by for Use.

To preserve Mulberries liquid.

TAKE two Quarts of Mulberry Juice, strain it, boil it over a gentle Fire, with a Pound and a half of Sugar till it become a Kind of Syrup; then slip into the Pan three Quarts of Mulberries not over ripe: Give them a Boil, then pour all into an Earthen Vessel, stop it closs, and keep it for Use.

Another Way.

BOIL the Sugar till a little pearled, allowing three Pounds to four Pounds of Mulberries, and give them a light covered Boiling in the same Sugar, shaking the Pan gently, then set it by till next Day, then drain off the Syrup in order to bring it to its pearled Quality; then slip in the Fruit, adding a little more pearled Sugar if needful: When cold enough, put it into Pots.

To preserve Seville *Oranges in Quarters, or in Sticks.*

EITHER zeast or turn your Oranges according as you design to do them, whether in Zeasts, Chips or Faggots. *Turning*, in this Sense, is a Term of Art which denotes a particular Manner of paring Oranges and

and Lemons, when the outer Rind or Peel is pared off very thin and narrow with a Knife for the Purpose, winding it about the Fruit, so as the Peel may extend to a very great Length without breaking. To *zeast*, is to cut the Peel from Top to Bottom in small Slips as thin as possible. The Orange thus prepared may be cut into Quarters, or into Sticks as you please. You must take away the inside Skin and the Juice; set them over the Fire in Water, do not put them in till the Water begins to boil, and when they are done enough, (which you will know by their slipping of a Pin when stuck into them) let them cool, and put them into fresh Water, and next into clarified Sugar; let them have seven or eight covered Boilings before you set them by to cool. Boil them over again till the Syrup is almost smooth; drain them next Day and put them into Pots, let your Syrup be pearled, and pour it on them. Keep them in that Way till you think fit to dry them.

Oranges preserved in Slips.

WHEN the Fruit is zeasted, cut the Pulp into Slips, which are to be slit again in their Thickness to make them very thin; scald these Slips in Water till they are very soft, then throw them into clarified Sugar newly passed thro' the straining Bag when it is ready to boil, and give it twenty Boilings: Next Day having brought your Sugar to the smooth Quality, put the Slips into it, and give them seven or eight Boilings: The third Day boil your Sugar till pearled, and give them a covered Boiling. Some Time after put them into Pots, and you may dry them as Occasion serves. Lemons, Limes and Citrons are preserved much the same Way, either intire, or in Sticks, Faggots, Zeasts, Slips, &c.

Red crisp Almonds, or Prawlings.

MELT a Pound of Loaf or powdered Sugar with a little Water, and let a Pound of Almonds be boiled in in it till they crackle; add as much Cocheneal as will give it a right red, let it boil again to its cracked Quality, and at that instant toss in your Almonds; and removing the Pan from the Fire, stir them close till they are dry. The Cocheneal may be prepared by boiling it with Allum and Cream of Tartar, which Liquor is generally used for every Thing that is to be brought to a fine Colour, as Marmalades, Jellies, Pastes, Creams, &c.

To preserve white Citrons.

CUT them in Pieces of what Size you please, put them in Salt and Water for four or five Hours; wash them and boil them tender, then drain them and put them into as much clarified Sugar as will cover them, and set them by till next Day; drain them and boil the Syrup a little smooth, when cool, put it on the Citrons; next Day boil your Syrup quite smooth, and pour it on the Citrons; the Day after boil all together, and put it into a Pot to be candied, or put in Jelly or Composts as you please. You must look over these Fruits so kept in Syrup, and if you perceive any Froth on them, give them a Boil; and if they should become very frothy and sour, boil first the Syrup, and then all together.

To make clear Quince Cakes.

BOIL and clarify over a Fire a Pint of the Syrup of Quinces, with a Quart or two of Raspberries; skim it well from time to time, add a Pound and a half of Sugar, and boil up the same Quantity of Sugar to a Candy Height, and pour it in hot; stir all together, and keep it close stirring till it is almost cold, then spread it upon Plates, and cut it into Cakes of what Shape you please.

Marmalade of Apricocks.

TAKE full ripe Apricocks, pare and quarter them, and take out the Strings; put three Quarters of a Pound of Loaf-sugar to every Pound of Apricocks, and put

put them into a pretty broad Pan; set the Aprieocks on the Fire without either Water or Sugar, keep them stirring that they may not burn: When they are melted and boiled a pretty while, strew in the Sugar as quick as you can, and let them boil quick till the Syrup is thick, and they look clear, then put them in Pots or Glasses.

Marmalade of Apples.

SCALD them in Water, and when tender take them out and drain them, and strain them through a Sieve; boil your Sugar till it is well feathered, allowing three Quarters of a Pound of Sugar to every Pound of Apples; temper and dry the whole over the Fire as usual, and let them simmer together; strew it over with fine Sugar, and put it into Pots or Glasses.

Marmalade of Raspberries.

MAKE the Body of this Marmalade of very ripe Currants, to which add a Handful of Raspberries, that it may look as it were all of Raspberries.

Marmalade of Quinces, after the Italian *Manner.*

PARE about thirty Quinces as thin as possible, and take out the Cores, and put them into a Quart of Water with two Pounds of Sugar, let all boil together till they are soft; then strain the Juice and Pulp, and put to it four Pounds of Sugar, and boil it up to a right Consistence.

To make Quiddany of Pipins, of an Amber or Ruby Colour.

PARE the Pipins, and cut them into Quarters, and boil them in as much Water as will cover them, till they are soft, and sink in the Water, then strain the Pulp. Take a Pint of the Liquor, and boil it with half a Pound of Sugar, till it appears a quaking Jelly on the Moulds. When the Quiddany is cold, turn it on a wet Trencher,

 and

and slide it into Boxes. If you would have it of a red Colour, let it boil leisurely, close covered, till it is red like Claret.

Quiddany of all Sorts of Plumbs.

BOIL the Plumbs in Apple Water till they are red as Claret; when you have made the Liquor strong of the Fruit, put to every Mutchkin half a Pound of Sugar, and let it boil till a Drop of it will hang on the Back of a Spoon like a quaking Jelly. If you would have it of an Amber Colour, you must boil it on a quick Fire.

Paste of ripe Apricocks.

APRICOCK Paste is made the same Way as the Marmalade, or you may scald the Apricocks without Sugar; but if they are not thoroughly ripe, bruise them well, or pound them in a Mortar. Then slip in the Fruit into an equal Quantity of cracked Sugar, and incorporated with it, when well dried over the Fire; then let all simmer, and dress your Paste as usual. You may dry it at the same Time if you please.

Goose-berry Paste.

TAKE them when full grown, wash them and put them into the preserving Pan, with as much Water as covers them; boil them very thick all to a Pommish; then strain them through a Hair Sieve into a Pan, and press out all the Juice; and, to every Pound of this Paste take one Pound and two Ounces of Sugar, boil it till it cracks; then mix in your Paste, and let it incorporate with Sugar over a slow Fire: When it is well incorporate, skim it, and fill your Pots, then skim it again, and when cold put it into the Stove. When it is crusted on the Top, turn them and set them in the Stove again, and when a little dry, cut them in long Pieces, and set them to dry quite; and when they are so crusted as to bear touching, turn them on Sieves, and dry the other Side, and put them into Boxes. You may make them

red

red or green, by putting the Colour, when the Sugar and Paste is all mixed, giving it a Warm all together.

To make Ketchup.

GET the largest Mushrooms, wipe them clean, and mash them with your Hand; strew on them a Handful of Salt; let them lye all Night, then put them on the Fire ten Minutes, keep them stirring all the while, then squeeze them through a Canvas, and let them settle; pour it from the Sediment, then put it on the Fire, and clarify it with the Whites of two Eggs; then put in it whole Pepper, Cloves, Mace, Ginger and *Jamaica* Pepper, and Salt; it must be very high seasoned: Boil one Part of it away, and when cold bottle it, putting the Spices in the Bottles with it.

To keep Artichoke Bottoms the whole Year.

PUT them in a Pot, and put as much Water about them as will cover them, salt them, let them boil till the Leaves come easily from them; then take off every thing of the Bottoms; put them in a slow Oven on or before the Fire; keep them in a dry Place, when they are thoroughly dry.

Syrup of Lemons and Oranges.

TO a Mutchkin of Juice put a Pound and a Half of fine Loaf Sugar; put it on the Fire and let it simmer, skim it, and stir it often, then let it settle; and when it is cold bottle it, but don't put the Sediment in it.

To preserve whole Oranges.

GRATE off the Rind very gently, cut a Bit out of the Top where the Stem is, and scoop out all that is in them; put them in a very clean Kettle of cold Water, cover it close, boil them as tender that you may thrust a Straw in them, shifting the Water three or four Times; then put them between two Cloaths to drain, and to every Pound of them put two Pounds of Loaf

Sugar

Sugar, with two Gills of Water, and boil it till it blows; ſkim it clean; then put in the Oranges, and boil them till they are very clear, keeping them down in the Syrup with a Spoon whil they are boiling: Then put them in Cans.

To preſerve Angelica.

BOIL the Stalks of Angelica in Water till they are very tender, then peel them and put them into other warm Water, and cover them till they are green'd on a gentle Fire: When they are green lay them on a Cloth to dry, and take their Weight of fine Sugar, and boil it to a Syrup; tye up the Stalks in any Shape you pleaſe, and boil them in the Syrup very quick; if you dry them, you muſt ſhake Sugar on them, and put them in a ſlow Oven.

To preſerve Peaches in Brandy.

PUT your Peaches in boiling Water, but don't let them boil; take them out and put them in Water, dry them between two Cloths, then put them in wide mouth'd Bottles; to ſix Peaches put a Quarter of a Pound of Sugar, clarify it, and put it on the Peaches, then fill up the Bottles with Brandy; ſtop them cloſs, and keep them in a cold Place.

To dry Pears or Apples.

TAKE preſerving Pears, and thruſt a wooden Skewer into the Head of them beyond the Core, then pare them the long Way, and ſcald them, but not too tender; then take their Weight of Sugar, and to every Pound of Sugar put two Gills of Water; clarify it, and put in your Pears; ſet them on the Fire, and let them boil very quick half an Hour, cover them with white Paper, and ſet them by till next Day. Then take them out of the Syrup, and boil it till it is thick and ropy; then put in the Pears, and put it on the Fire, and let the Syrup boil very faſt over them: Then cover them with Paper, and ſet them in the Oven, or

Stove

Stove for twenty-four Hours; then take it out, and put them on a Sieve; then lay them on White-iron Plates, and duſt them with fine Sugar, then put them in the Oven; and when one Side is dry lay them on Papers, and turn them, and duſt the other with Sugar; ſqueeze the Pears by Degrees. If you do Apples, ſqueeze the Eyes to the Stalks: When they are dry put them in Boxes, with Papers between. You may do Apricocks, Peaches and Nectarines the ſame Way; but when they are ſcalded take out the Stones.

CHAP. VI.

Of WINES, &c.

To make Orange Wine.

TO ſix Gallons of Water, put twelve Pounds of ſingle refined Sugar, the Whites of four Eggs well beaten, put them in the cold Water; then let it boil three Quarters of an Hour, taking off the Scum as it riſes; when it is cold put in two Spoonfuls of Barm, and ſix Ounces of Syrup of Lemons beaten together; put in alſo the Juice and Rinds of fifty Oranges thin pared, that no white Part, or any of the Seeds go in with the Juice which ſhould be ſtrained: Let all ſtand two Days in an open Veſſel, or large Pan, then put it in a cloſs Veſſel, and in three or four Days ſtop it down. When it has ſtood three Weeks then draw it off into another Veſſel, and add to it two Quarts of Rheniſh or white Wine. Then ſtop it cloſs again, and in ſix Weeks it will be fine to bottle, and to drink in a Month after. Obſerve, that an *Engliſh* Gallon is two *Scots* Pints, and, if the Barm be not very good, to put in thirteen or fourteen Sp[illegible]fuls

To make Raisin Wine.

TO each five Pounds of Raisins picked clean from the Stalks, take one *English* Gallon of cold Water; chop the Raisins small, and put them into a Vessel, fit for the Quantity; then pour on the cold Water, stir them about, and cover the Vessel with a Cloth, so let them stand ten Days, stirring them about twice a-day: At the End of ten Days, strain out the Liquor through a Search, squeezing the Raisins very well; then put the Liquor into a Barrel that will just hold the Quantity you make. After a hissing Noise, which is commonly about three Weeks after, bung up the Barrel, and let it stand a Year, then bottle it for Use.

To make Vinegar.

TAKE half the Quantity of the above Water, let it be boiling hot, and pour it upon the Raisins: After you have squeezed them out of the first Liquor, and after standing, (till it is as cold as Wort, when Barm is put to it) take a Mutchkin of good Barm and put to it, and let it work two Weeks, stirring it once or twice a-day; then squeeze it through a Search into a Barrel, and set it by a Fire: When it has wrought a Fortnight in the Barrel, bung it up, and let it stand till sour enough, which will be according to the Degree of Heat; and in eight or ten Months it is commonly done.

To make Balm Wine.

TO every Chopin of Honey, put three Chopins of Water; boil it on a quick Fire, till one Chopin is boiled away; take Care to keep it close skimmed, then put it to cool, and put in it a large Handful of Balm; when almost cold, put in it half a Gill of the best Barm, and let it stand till the Head is flat, and done working, which will be in four or five Days; then skim it, and strain it through a very fine Search in a Can, but take Care that the Grounds at the Bottom do not mix with it; put it in a Jar, and stop it close, and when

cle-

clear, bottle it; it will keep ſeven or eight Years; the older the better. You may make Elder Wine the ſame Way of the white Bloſſom, but take Care that none of the Stems or green be among them. They both are very wholeſome. Meath is made the ſame Way, leaving out the Balm and Elder Flowers.

To make Metheglin.

GET ſome good ſtrong Wort, and to every four Chopins of it, put a Chopin of Honey; boil one Chopin away on a quick Fire, keep it well ſkimmed, and when cold, put a Gill of Barm to it, and let it work two or three Days, then put it in your Caſk; a Brandy one is beſt for all Wines, if you make a Quantity of them: Get a Bag of Linen, and to every *Engliſh* Gallon, put in it two Nutmegs; cut in Quarters a Quarter of an Ounce of Ginger, one Dram of Mace, one of Cloves groſly pounded; put the Bag with theſe in it, in the Caſk; bottle it in ſix Months, or you may not till twelve.

To make Currant Wine, white or red.

TAKE the Currants when they are full ripe, and ſqueeze them through a coarſe Cloth, and put to every *Engliſh* Gallon of Juice, two Gallons of boiled ſoft Water, and three Pounds of Sugar; ſtir it very well together, then barrel it up, filling up the Barrel every Day, till it has done working; then bung it up cloſe, and let it ſtand ſix Months, and bottle it. Brandy Caſks are beſt for all Sorts of made Wine.

To make Gooſe-berry Wine.

GATHER the Gooſe-berries in dry Weather when they are half ripe, bruiſe them in a Tub with a wooden Mallet or Peſtle; then put them in a coarſe Canvas Bag, and preſs out all the Juice; to every *Engliſh* Gallon put three Pounds of powdered Sugar, ſtir the Sugar in it till it diſſolves, then put it in a Caſk; and if you make

but

but a ſmall Quantity, put it in a ſmall Caſk, for it muſt be full; let it ſtand three Weeks, then draw it off, and pour out the Lees; then put it again in the Caſk and ſtop it cloſe, then let it ſtand three Months and bottle it: If you make a large Quantity, let it ſtand longer in the Caſk; if you ſqueeze a Dozen of bitter Oranges in it, and put ſome of the Rinds pared thin in it, they will give it a fine Taſte.

Elder-berry Wine.

GATHER the Elder-berries when they are full ripe, when it is a very dry Day; then bruiſe them with your Hands and ſtrain them, then ſet the Liquor by in a Gray-beard for twelve Hours to ſettle; then put to every Pint of the Juice, a Pint and a half of Water; and to every *Engliſh* Gallon of this Liquor, put three Pounds of *Liſbon* Sugar; put it in a Kettle on the Fire, and when it is almoſt boiling, clarify it with the Whites of four Eggs; let it boil an Hour, and when it is almoſt cold, put in it a little ſtrong Ale Barm, and then ton it; and as it works out, fill up the Veſſel with ſome of the ſame Liquor; in a Month's Time it will be fit to be bottled; and after it is bottled, it will be fit to drink in two Months; but remember that all Liquors muſt be fine before they are bottled: When it is fine, it will be the better to put in it a Bottle of Mountain Wine.

To make purging Ale.

TAKE Polypody of the Oak and Senna, of each two Ounces, of Sarſaparilla an Ounce, Aniſe-ſeeds and Carraway Seeds, of each half an Ounce; ſix Handfuls of Scurvy-graſs, three of Ground-ivy, one of Agrimony, and one of Maiden-hair; beat all theſe eaſily, and put them in a coarſe Canvas Bag, and hang them in a Gallon of ſtrong Ale that is juſt working, and it will be fit to drink in five or ſix Days.

To brew ſtrong Ale and ſmall Beer.

BOIL the Water, and put ſome of the Malt in the Vat, and ſtir it and the boiling Water very well together; then put in more Malt and more Water maſhed pretty thin; then cover the Vat and let it ſtand three Hours; then let ſome of the Wort run, and throw it up again once or twice till it is clear; ſtrew ſome dry Malt on the Top of the Vat; put your Hops in the Tub that the Wort runs in, and then put them in the brewing Pan on the Fire with the Wort; let it boil till it curdles, and then clears; put boiling Water on the Vat by Degrees. Twenty *Engliſh* Buſhels of Malt will make two Hogſheads of ſtrong Ale, and four Hogſheads of ſmall Beer, but it will take ten Pounds of Hops. This Ale will keep two or three Years; when it is almoſt as cold as Water, barm it, but ſtrain the Hops out of it when it is warm, and boil them in the ſmall Beer: Let it work three Days, then ſkim it and barrel it, and when it is done working ſtop it up cloſs, but keep the Barrel always filling while it is working. *October* or *March* is the beſt Time to brew.

To make Syder.

WHEN the Apples are ripe, pull them on a dry Day, and pound them in a Trough with wooden Pounders, then put them in a Hair Bag, and preſs the Juice out of them; put it in a Brandy or white Wine Caſk that is very ſweet: Put in the Caſk ſome Slices of Apples, and two Penny-worth of Iſinglaſs; ſtop the Bung cloſs, and bottle it in ten Months.

To make Ratafia.

TAKE three Gallons of Brandy, or good Whiſky, and blanch and pound half a Pound of bitter Almonds, and put them in the Spirits, with the Rind of Lemons. Let them infuſe a Fortnight, then filter off the Spirits, and cork the Bottles close you put it in; it is good for any Puddings.

To distill cold Surfeit Water.

TAKE two Handfuls of Spearmint, two of Balm, one of Angelica, one of Wormwood, one of Carduus, and one of Marigold Flowers; cut them, and put them in Water, then wring them out, and put them in the Still. Keep wet Cloths about it, and a slow Fire under it.

To make Plague Water.

TAKE Rue, Carduus, Balm, Spearmint, Wormwood, Penny-royal, Dragon, Marigold Flowers, Angelica and Rosemary, of each two Handfuls; cut them small, and put them in the Still with Anise-seeds, Carraway, Coriander, and sweet Fennel Seeds; then cover them with Spirits, and distill it off.

To make Shrub.

TAKE five *English* Gallons of Rum, three Chopins of Orange and Lemon-juice, and four Pounds of double refined Sugar; mix all together, but first pare the Rind of some of the Lemons and Oranges, and let them infuse in the Rum for six Hours: Let all run through a Jelly-bag, then cask it till it is fine, and bottle it.

A very fine Wash for Ladies that have the Scurvy, or any Redness in the Face.

BOIL two Ounces of fine Barley, a Chopin of Water to four Gills, beat two Ounces of Almonds to a Paste, mixing them with a little of the Barley Water; when cold, warm them, and squeeze them through a Cloth; then dissolve one Penny-worth of Camphire in a Spoonful of Brandy, or any strong Spirits: Mix them and wash the Face every Night when you are going

ing to Bed: It is the beſt Waſh ever was made for the Face.

The beſt Pomatum for the Lips.

TAKE an Ounce of Sperma-cete, and mix it with an Ounce of the Oil of bitter Almonds, and a little pounded Cocheneal; melt them all together and ſtrain it through a Cloth in a little Roſe-water, and rub your Lips going to Bed at Night.

To make Eye-Water.

GET two Gills of white Roſe water, put in it the Bigneſs of a Nut of white Vitriol, and the ſame Quantity of the fineſt Loaf-ſugar; when it is diſſolved ſhake the Bottle, and waſh the Eyes going to Bed with it, and a ſoft clean Cloth: It is as good an Eye-Water as ever was made.

To make the Sacred Tincture.

PUT in a Mutchkin Bottle five Penny-worth of Hiera Picra, one of Cocheneal pounded; then fill the Bottle with Half *Lisbon* Wine, and Half Brandy, tye a Bit of clean Cloth on the Bottle, and put it in a Pan of cold Water, as full that it won't go into the Bottle; put it on a very ſlow Fire, and don't let it boil but ſimmer; then take off the Pan, and let the Bottle ſtand till the Water is cold: It is a very ſafe gentle Phyſick, and good for a Cholick.

To make Stoughton's *Drops.*

INFUSE in a Chopin of *French* Brandy a Penny-worth of Cocheneal, a Penny-worth of Snake-root, half an Ounce of *Jamaica* Oranges, two Ounces of bitter Orange-peel, one Ounce of Gentian-root, two Drachms of *Turkey* Rhubarb; pound the Rhubarb, Cocheneal, and *Jamaica* Oranges, ſlice the Gentian; put them near the Fire for two Days in a ſtrong Glaſs Bottle; then put the Bottle in a Pan of cold Water, on a ſlow

ſlow Fire: And when it ſimmers take off the Pan, and when the Water is cold take out the Bottle, let it ſtand two Days; then pour off all that is clear, and you may put ſtrong Whiſkey to the reſt, and it will be good for preſent Uſe.

To make Daffy's *Elixir.*

TAKE a Mutchkin of Brandy, and a Mutchkin of *Liſbon;* infuſe in it half an Ounce of Carraway, half an Ounce of Aniſe-ſeed, half an Ounce of ſweet Fennel-ſeeds, one Ounce of Hiera-picra, one Ounce of bitter Alloways, two Drachms of Saffron, two Ounces of bitter Orange-peel, and one of Snake-root; let theſe ly near the Fire for a Fortnight, then put the Bottle in a Pan of cold Water, and when it ſimmers take it off; when cold filter it off: You may take two Spoonfuls of it at Night, it is good for a Cholick, and is a gentle Phyſick.

To make the yellow Balſam.

TAKE four Pounds of *May* Butter, and gather in a dry Day a Pound of Elder Flowers, let none of the Stems or Green be in them; mix them with the Butter in a cloſs well glazed Can; put it in the Sun by Day, and near the Fire by Night; keep them that Way till the green Broom bloſſoms; then get a Pound of the Bloſſoms, and mix them very well together; keep them as above for five or ſix Weeks; then warm it well, but don't boil it, and wring it all out in a Cloth as well as you can. It is good for any Inflammation, Pain or Stitch, rubbing the Part affected before the Fire with a very little of it; and if inwardly, ſwallow five or ſix Pills roll'd in Sugar: It is as wholeſome and ſafe a Thing as ever was taken.

FINIS.

Made in the USA
Middletown, DE
19 July 2020